ROCKIN' THE FRONT PORCH

SHARING THE FAITH IN THE NEW NORMAL

Marie,
friend, comrade,
and life-line,
thank you for
always being there.

Jake Jacobson

HAROLD "JAKE" JACOBSON

(next time you get asked about
evangelism, just tell them, "you
know the author.")

ISBN: 978-1-7168-9317-9 (sc)
ISBN: 978-1-7168-9316-2 (e)

Lulu Publishing Services rev. date: 06/04/2020

CONTENTS

DEDICATION

This book is dedicated to my faithful Front Porch companions: To Pastor Stephen Bouman, who was crazy enough to take a chance on me. To Pastor Erika Uthe, who encouraged me to take a walk off the Front Porch with this book. To the members of the Evangelism Task Force of the Evangelical Lutheran Church in America: Danielle Denise, Rick Carter, Rob James, Elise Rothfusz, Matt Short, Julianne Smith, Keith Zeh and to all my fellow Directors for Evangelical Mission, both past and present, for taking time to sit on the porch with me and share their stories of faith. Also, to the congregations of Faith Lutheran Church (White Oak, PA) and St. Paul's Lutheran Church (Neenah, WI) for their willingness to embrace this work and assist in the writing of this book.

AUTHOR'S NOTE

As I put the finishing touches on this book, the world is locked down by the COVID-19 virus pandemic. As churches have been forced to discontinue gathering for worship they have turned to the internet. I have also taken my rocking chair to a virtual porch and done some Front Porchin' there. The response was overwhelming. There is such a hunger for the hope that one finds in our Story (especially among those who are not regular attenders in our churches).

Where the church will be when this pandemic passes, is anyone's guess but the desire to learn and listen to the Story once again has been resurrected like a valley of old, dry bones. I believe learning to share that Story is more critical than ever and new and exciting avenues are just being tested. (see also Appendix E for more thoughts on a theological frame to look at evangelism in this "new normal").

Harold "Jake" Jacobson
April 2020

PREFACE

I met Chris his first year at Clarion University of PA at a midsemester cookie break sponsored by campus ministry. He was there with his roommate who had become a regular at Grace's worship. Chris and I hit it off from the moment we met. We found connections and mutual interests galore. We sat and talked for several hours. On my way back home, I remarked to myself that I would probably see Chris in church on Sunday. (I was still young and naïve enough to believe that people came to church because of the pastor – age and experience has changed that thinking).

That Sunday there was no Chris. Weeks went by, months went by, semesters went by, years went by and still no Chris. We met regularly on campus and we saw each other in town but never in church. Then on the last Sunday of his senior year I looked up and saw Chris and his roommate sitting in the back pew. I figured he came just to say goodbye.

You can imagine my surprise when the following Sunday he was there without his roommate. He had also hung behind after service to talk with me. "Pastor, I want to join the church." Somewhat shocked, I replied, "Give me a call this week and we can set up a time to get started on the process." He didn't call.

The next week he was waiting for me after church once again. "Pastor Jake, I needed to tell you something, but I couldn't do it over the phone. I'm kind of embarrassed ... I've never been baptized." "That's ok, baptism will be the way we welcome you into the church. Give me a call this week and we can set up a time to get started on the process." He didn't call.

Chris was not there the next Sunday, or the Sunday after that, or the Sunday after that. In fact, Chris seemed to be MIA. I figured I must have said something to scare him off or upset him. About the time I had given myself a good beating up there he was waiting for me after church. "I bet you wondered what happened to me?"

"I decided that if I wanted to become a Christian, I should make sure what kind of Christian I wanted to be. So, I visited all the churches in town. I want to be a Lutheran Christian."

"Fine, be in my office tomorrow morning at 9:00." He was.

We began to talk about his story and how he had gotten to Clarion and how he had come to his decision to join the church. I began to talk about the Bible, sharing some of the important stories. He hung with me through the Old Testament but as we reached the New Testament, he became more agitated. I noticed it, but since he was my first adult baptism and I had so much good stuff I wanted to share, I kept plowing on until he had had enough. "Pastor Jake, shut up, I have a question. You keep talking about this Jesus guy. Who is Jesus?"

Who is Jesus? I want you to take a few moments for that to sink in and then think about how different your lives would be if you had never heard about Jesus. What would your world look like without Jesus?

Thirty years ago, Chris was an exception. Today, Chris is the norm.

INTRODUCTION

When I was growing up in a tiny Southwestern New York town my favorite space in all the world was the front porch (Today we would call it a three-season room). There on an old daybed (so old that you had to watch out for protruding springs) I would watch the world go by, lose myself in a good book or engage in my favorite past-time… dreaming.

Front porches were dramatic and magical places for me. It was my grandmother's front porch that storied me into the world of unconditional love that waited in her arms every time I went to visit. It was the front porch of my Uncle George with its big wooden rockers that storied me into a larger family context as my cousin and I "overheard" the family stories. It was my Aunt Marie's porch and the nightly conversations that storied me from a little boy into a young man. It was the front porch of Fred Hagman's house (formerly my Jacobson grandparents' house) that storied me in the coming of my family from Sweden. It was on the front steps of Stevens Hall at Gettysburg College that I was storied into a budding theologian. It was Henry Slicker's wrap-around porch that looked down on Main Street that I was storied into the life of a new community. It is my present front porch where I am storied into reclamation and renewal as I enjoy a good book and a pipe.

In addition to all these actual porches in my life there are many figurative porches that story my life. There are Michelle's Coffee Shoppe, Walmart, Main Street, the football stadium, the baseball field and the basketball bleachers to mention but a few.

When I was first called as an Assistant to the Bishop, I was told my duties would be forming faith and making disciples. My previous work in the adult catechumenate made this work a natural fit. Within a year my position radically changed, and my portfolio now includes evangelism and stewardship. While I had done well for 25 years successfully avoiding those two topics in the parish, suddenly I was called to be the resident expert. I did what I always do when faced with such a challenge I started reading everything I could on the subject. But I found that there was little that was applicable to my setting in small-town and rural ministry. I also discovered that every time I mentioned the word evangelism people's eyes glazed over or they left the room. So, I decided that I needed a new word and a better process. It was then that I remembered **that** day.

It was *that* day, that great and terrible day, September 11, 2001. The events of the day had left me mentally and physically drained. I went to my place of refreshment in those days – my sky chair on the front porch. One of the characteristics of my neighborhood is that we all have front porches and use them often. On that night all the front porches of the neighborhood were occupied. It seemed that we were being driven into community. In what I've called the blowing of the Divine Dog Whistle we all began to migrate one by one to Peg's front porch. Peg was the matriarch of the neighborhood and regularly entertained the neighborhood conversations from her porch.

We all gathered there including the college students next door. The conversation quickly settled in on the day's events. We took turns rehearsing where we were when we first heard the news, when we saw the footage of the plane crashing into the towers, and when we realized that we were not witnessing an accident but an act of terror. We then began to talk about those friends and loved ones we had not heard from… those in harm's way… we wondered what it would mean for our children… Peg's son-in-law was working in the Pentagon and my boys were of an age that conjured up vivid memories of the draft of the Vietnam era.

What I noticed was that before long the language being used in our conversation was faith talk. It was as if the only language strong enough to hold the content of that day was the language of faith. During this evolving conversation one of the college students (who had earlier admitted that he never darkened the door of a church) chimed up with, "I only have one question that I want an answer for and that is, 'Where in the hell was God this morning?'"

For the next several hours there on the front porch we engaged that question in holy conversation. This was not a time for pious platitudes or trite religious answers… it was a roll up your sleeves and get down and dirty in practical theology. As I reflected on that night several months later, I realized that we were beginning to do the work of post-9/11 hermeneutics. What does this all mean in light of our faith?

No one said we had to go out and be neighborly on that dark night. It simply grew out of the deep need we felt – a need to be in community. What happened that night (after we had wrung out the emotion of the day in our rehearsal and questioning) was a profound story-ing of our life together as residents of these United States, the community of Clarion **and** the community of the Kingdom of God. These were not inherently religious folk that wandered back and forth that night, but the language of faith was the only language to adequately carry the weight of what had and was happening to us.

I believe that the front porches of our lives offer to us a *natural* context for such story-ing that can serve as the vehicle for what we traditionally refer to as evangelism.

This book offers some preliminary thoughts from my Front Porch… as to how we might more intentionally share the story of our faith as we discover it anew on the Front Porches of our lives. It is divided into three sections:

Part 1: **Front Porchin',**

A process of sharing our faith both among the faithful as well as those who we encounter in the world.

Part 2: **Transforming Grace**

An implementation of Front Porchin' as a process of transformation and conversion.

Part 3: **Building a Mission Table**

A comprehensive planning tool to help congregations identify and utilize their Front Porches.

PART 1

FRONT PORCHIN'

CHAPTER 1

FRONT PORCHIN'

Peg and Joe (now of blessed memory), and their grown daughter Peggy Jo were my neighbors for over 30 years. One of the rites of spring at their house was the cleaning of the front porch, the bringing out of the porch furniture and the planting of the flower boxes that line the porch. The rite is carried out with hopeful anticipation and faithful precision. When all was made ready and the weather turned warm you would find them seated there every evening until the night fell around them. They hosted a wide circle of friends and family as well as the occasional pedestrian passerby. I knew that sometime over the course of those months between May and November I would be drawn at least once to spend an evening on that porch. It didn't seem to matter how much time had passed between those visits we would pick up the pieces of our life together as though there was never an absence.

Why? What makes this possible? I have spent many a night wondering, and I believe that I am beginning to gain some clarity. We share a story. It is a story that includes children and grandchildren, hopes, dreams, fears and griefs. It is the thread of that shared story that gets picked up and weaves us back together as front porch neighbors.

Stories are important. One of the funny stories about Peg's hospitality that I learned after her death was that even though she would fuss all over those who passed by with dogs, Peg personally disliked dogs. Her dislike of dogs however was overruled by her love of the story and the people who shared them. Stories are important. Forty years ago, the Lutheran Church in America introduced a program called *Word and Witness*. While its vision was powerful it lacked the clarity of methodology necessary to have the desired impact on the church. One of the keys to that program was the three-fold image of story-ing: God's story, My story, Your story.

According to the program it is where the three stories intersect that faith sharing occurs. Or as I have come to describe it – that's where Front Porchin' happens.

As I shared earlier, my front porch growing up was an enclosed three-season porch. It was there on the day bed that I would curl up and read for hours on end. It was in that time of daydreaming that I was story-ed into mysteries of a world beyond my tiny and limited existence. We begin our "porch-work" with the nurturing of the mysteries of our faith. The starting point is our prayer life – both personal and corporate. To be an evangelist or an evangelizing congregation we need to continually check in with the God that has called us into being. This means a daily devotional life and a sense of corporate prayer life as the congregation.

With prayer comes the regular and intentional encountering of God's story. Again, we engage in this encounter both within our personal reading of scripture and the corporate experiencing of the Word in worship, preaching, sacrament and gathered body. Together, these contexts provide a front porch for God to re-story our lives in light of God's story. As we become steeped in this story we will find that it is not about us telling others about Jesus as it is revealing to others the Jesus that is embodied in our lives, individually and corporately.

Memorial Day preparations in my family were a multi-day and two-state affair. As I look back on those trips, I find that much of my understanding of my place in the world of family was discovered and nurtured in the stories told between the generations as we tended graves and drove between grave sites. Two stops along the way were my Uncle George's and Fred and Anna Hagman's front porches. As the adults enjoyed a repast of cookies and tea on my Uncle George's front porch, my cousin Joanne and I would position our "playing" in such a way that we were able to overhear the stories of family told. (We probably heard stories that we were not meant to hear). In a similar fashion I would listen intently on the Hagman's porch as dad and Fred shared stories of Fred and my grandfather, my Uncle Art and the cast of infamous Jacobson's that were dead long before I was born.

In much the same way, as we gather around Word and Sacrament, we overhear the story of God and are story-ed by it. The first task of this strategy will be to immerse the congregation and participants, through daily scripture reading and intentional Bible study, in the story of God as we have received it through the Word made flesh, Jesus Christ.

The second task, and the place where I believe we diverted the intention of *Word and Witness*, is to internalize God's story in such a way that we see how God's story and My story are not separate stories but rather one that shines through the other.

I was adopted into my present family at the age of 9 months. Their story is not *my* story and yet through the front porches of their lives they have helped me to see that I have been grafted into that story so that to envision telling my story without that larger family story is impossible. How do we tell our story in such a way that God's story speaks in, with and under that story of our lives?

The third task will be the intentional sharing of that story with one another in a non-threatening way so that we become more comfortable with our story and the telling of it. In a sense what we are talking about is *evangelical socialization*. At an early age my Aunt Marie swept me across the street and into the world of her front porch. I was her day-laborer as she attended a myriad of flowers and crops. When we finished a day's work, we would sit on her porch swing with cookies and milk. It was there that I learned to talk with adults about what I believed and felt. It was there that I learned to ask questions about God and life. She was not threatened by my thousand and one questions and created a safe place to talk about those things. Our task is to build up our front porches so that we provide such a context for the Spirit to bring Our/God's story and Your story into dialog.

The common misconception behind most of our evangelism efforts these days is that all we need to do is to tell people about Jesus and they will "get it." How much effort has been spent on well-meaning efforts to teach the Bible in our congregations? However, as we produce study resources, interpretive pieces, we write *about* Jesus, we pursue the historical Jesus... but are we any closer to answering the question? Who is this Jesus?

I believe the answer can be found in the Greek...I mean Greeks.

Those Greeks who come to Philip in John's gospel and ask, "Sir, we wish to see Jesus." Note. They do not demand, "Tell us about Jesus!" They ask to **see** Jesus for themselves. This was the question that had led my college student to seek baptism…I want to see Jesus! It is for this that those who come within the walls of our churches and gather with us outside of them are seeking. Even if they don't know it! This raises for us two dilemmas: "Have we ever **seen/encountered** Jesus?" and "How do we **embody** Jesus in such a way that someone else can see him?"

As Chris and I began to work together on discovering who Jesus is, it became quite clear that Chris was not interested in Jesus 101 (which was a great disappointment because I had so much stuff from college and seminary that I could dazzle him with). Instead he informed me that he wanted to meet the Jesus that I knew. He wanted to get to know the Jesus that stood with me when I preached and led worship. He wanted to become acquainted with the Jesus that got me through the everyday stuff of life. In short, he wanted to hear my story of life with Jesus.

We have been steeped in a tradition that has taught us about Jesus but at least in the last half century has not done well with inviting us into an encounter with Jesus. Now, as we face declining attendance, bare Sunday School rooms, and larger budget deficits we want to know, "How do we do evangelism?" Truthfully, the question is more like, "How can we get more people in the pews, more money in the plate and children to fill our Sunday Schools?" If it is all about the "butts and bucks," we might as well stop. Any gains will be short-lived. There is no magic bullet.

Making Disciples/evangelism is hard work these days because no one is going to help us (in fact society is working against us). It is also hard because it requires a whole shift in our thinking and our way of being church. It calls for intentionality. It takes more than sprucing up the grounds and making sure a visitor can find their way around our churches (if one might stumble in by accident). It requires intentional faith formation - both on the part of the pastor and congregation as well as those who come to become part of the church. It is not rocket science but rather a return to the ABC's of the church. It means taking advantage of our front porch and the activity that occurs there. This book will look at the story-ing process as well as how to better utilize the front porch opportunities in our churches and our lives.

A note on "story" before we begin: My preaching tends to be anecdotal and every so often someone (often one of my children) asks, "Was that story you told really true?" My answer is always, "Yes, but that doesn't mean that if the others in the story were asked to tell the same story that it might not be different." Truth does not always demand factuality. This also applies not only to My Story and Your Story but also God's Story. It has only been since the age of Enlightenment that we have been concerned by factuality and accuracy. This has spilled over into our study of God's Story. The search for the historical Jesus that began around the turn of the 20th Century has given way to the Jesus Project of the turn of the 21st Century (and all of this in being "discovered" by the Evangelicals of today with fresh enthusiasm). Neither movement has provided satisfactory answers to those who wish to rationalize scripture. As my organic chemistry lab partner in college once challenged me, "Show me where Adam's sons wives came from in the Bible and I will believe in God!" The Bible's truth is not in its factuality but in its witness to the living God. It is a truth that shapes us as God's people as we strive to live together.

CHAPTER 2

PROCESS

In both the Hebrew Scriptures (Isaiah 43:10) and the New Testament (Acts 1:8) the announcement is made to God's faithful people that they are to "be my [*God/Christ*] witnesses." The thought of witnessing strikes fear into the boldest Christian. In an instant our blood goes cold and our knees go weak…and parts of our body tighten up!"

It is at this point in my work that I usually pause and invite those I am working with to join me in a relaxation exercise. I invite them to close their eyes and begin to take some slow deep breaths. After a minute of this I let them know that I will be giving them three words and that I want them to fasten on to the first thing that comes into their mind when they hear those words. It may be an image, a song, a piece of scripture, a person… or something else. Once they have that, I encourage them to sit with it. The three words are: Jesus, loves, me. I give them a couple of minutes to focus their thoughts and then I ask them to turn to the person next to them and share what came to mind. I have yet to work with a group where I have not had difficulty bringing them back from their conversations. (This has led me to the conclusion that our people are not reluctant to share their faith stories but rather have not been given permission or a structure in which to do so).

Returning to our model, I point out that they have just engaged in faith sharing: they have shared a part of their story (image) which had to do with God's story (Jesus loves me) with another person and their faith story. The process is as simple as that.

My Story. Spoken or unspoken we bring to any sharing of stories our own story. Our hopes and dreams, anxieties and fears, the events of our lives and the world we have lived in have shaped who we are and more importantly how we see ourselves. What is your story? In chapter 3 I will propose some exercises to help us better understand our stories and the impact those stories will have as we seek to share our lives of faith with others.

God's Story. It is not just any story that we are called to share as evangelists but rather we have been called to share the Good News of God's faithful revelation in Christ Jesus. Do we know that story? I believe that our fear of evangelism grows out of our conception that one needs an "expert" to understand Scripture. If we truly believe that we cannot come to Christ by our own reason or strength but only through the gift of the Holy Spirit, then at some point we need to start relying on that gift instead of settling for our own inabilities. Note: it is only after the Pentecost in the Book of the Acts of the Apostles that the apostles (those *sent ones*) are in fact empowered to share the good news. That said we must be diligent in our study of scripture and avail ourselves to this saving Word. In chapter 4 I will propose a course of study to help congregations overhear Scripture without being overwhelmed by it.

God's Story/My Story. The critical failure of much of what we call Bible Study is that it becomes a head trip. We learn *about* the Bible. The Bible is sacramental in that it points beyond itself to God. The purpose of having scripture is not that we come to know **it** but rather that we are invited into a deeper relationship with that God that we call, Father, Son and Holy Spirit. So often the prophets were called to "eat" the Word of God before going to proclaim it. How do we eat and digest this Word, sweeter than honey, that we have been given in such a way that we begin to see our life story within the context of God's good news? Chapter 5 will deal with eating habits.

My Story/Your Story. One of the problems with" program evangelism" is that it cares little for the nature of who it is that you are called to share the good news with apart from the sense of a target audience. If we affirm in our theology the dignity of each human being as one created in the image of God (Genesis 1:26) then we are called to treat those to whom we are sent with that dignity. This means that we enter into relationship with

7

them. We come to know their story and share our story. How else can we possibly know in what way to share God's story with them in such a way that it becomes truly good news? Chapter 6 will offer help in intentional listening and story-ing.

My Story/Your Story/God's Story. Finally, we reach the object of our journey as those who have been sent. Did I tell you that this work of evangelization is not a *quick* fix? In Chapter 7 I will share two models of evangelization: spiritual direction and the catecumenate. Both processes offer us insights how to approach the integral task of evangelization or perhaps better said, making disciples and forming faith.

CHAPTER 3

MY STORY

I grew up in a town where it wasn't terribly important for me to know my story because everyone in town knew my story. They knew my parents and my grandparents. They remembered when I was brought home for adoption. It mattered little what I envisioned of myself for they were ready to redefine and correct any misconceptions of myself that I might have (How many of our congregations function in a similar way?). If asked to tell my story I learned to defer to the community.

In startling contrast, the congregation in which I was raised (which was not in my hometown) was a place where I was free and encouraged to explore who I was as a child of God. While my mother and father were well known, assumptions about me were not made (at least not shared with me). I had my own identity. Even if I did not know who I was yet they seemed to be in no hurry to pronounce judgments or assign attributes. I was given space to grow and explore apart from my parents and never did I ever feel that I was just a child. There was a sense of importance (sacredness) in my simply being who I was. Looking back, I realize how important that experience was in shaping my life of faith. This is the atmosphere that we need to create as we seek to encourage the construction and telling of our stories.

How do we do this work of construction? Many of us have had the experience of ice breakers that have asked us to share who we are and found ourselves stuttering and stammering or searching what of me is of any interest to these people? As hard as it is culturally for us to focus on ourselves it is a critical piece of this process to understand who we are or better how we see ourselves as children of God and our life as a journey with that God.

On a day in June, exactly 62 years to the day of my birth, my biological mother and I were reunited. It was an incredibly emotional moment for both of us. On that day the thread of the narrative was picked up again and the two of us began a process of learning to sing a new song in this strange and wonderful place we now find ourselves in.

While I have spent a lifetime constructing a narrative that I could live with now I am confronted with a new version of that story and the challenge of weaving it into the previous story of my life. While my old story began: My mother gave me up for adoption after trying to keep me until I was adopted by my new parents at 9 months of age. My new story begins: My 16-year-old mother was sexually assaulted by my 30-year-old sexual predator father. She was placed in a hospital facility for unwed mothers. Upon birthing me I was immediately taken from her and placed in a nursery. No one knows of my whereabouts between birth and adoption. The decision to adopt was my father's and the cost to my mother both professionally and personally was very high. She exacted that price out on me regularly. When I was 10 my father was diagnosed with terminal cancer and died three years later.

I share this because as we begin this work of personal narrative it is often a difficult and emotional story to tell even to ourselves. We must be patient with ourselves and those who are also doing this work.

We begin the process of developing our faith story by graphing our lives. Where are the highs and lows in the story?

Did you find turning points along your graph? One of the phenomena that I have observed with this process over the years is that regularly some comes to me and says, "I thought this was the darkest time of my life but looking at it in this perspective I see that if it had not happened not of the rest of the things in my life would have gone in the same way and I wouldn't want to give those up. So, I guess it is both a low and a high."

I ask the participants to see if they can identify any patterns. Are there trends or themes present in their story? As I looked at my story the first time, I did this exercise, I was shocked at how much of my young life was dominated by loss and death. Not only the personal losses but the communal losses of national figures like John F. Kennedy, Robert Kennedy, Martin Luther King Jr. as well as the Vietnam War. That colored my story greatly... it was a story of great loss.

What did you include and what did you choose to leave out? Depending on your age there simply is not enough room to include it all so how did you choose what to include and what to edit?

These stories are sacred and holy things. For this reason, I encourage that the debriefing of them remain general and voluntary. Questions like: Were there any 'ah ha' discoveries? Did you discover patterns? How do you see your story differently? are appropriate. I also encourage participants to take their stories home and keep them in a safe or holy place (a devotional Bible is an appropriate dwelling place). I ask them to periodically take they our and review them, pray with them, and perhaps even rewrite them.

Naomi Carlson was a member of my home congregation and personally supported me both in prayer and finance through seminary. Ni had an uncanny way of knowing when I needed both gifts most. As such it was not a surprise on one of my visits to Emanuel to lead worship that she said, "Harold, I have something to give you after worship." It turned out to be her father's Swedish Bible. Having no remaining family, she gave it to me because she knew of no one else to entrust it with. A year or so later I led the congregation through a Front Porchin' experience. A week after the event I received in the mail Naomi's timeline (obviously carefully reworked and carefully annotated). There was a sticky note on it that simply read, "Harold, I thought you should know my story." Six months later Naomi Carlson died.

As I looked back on those events, I realized that Naomi handed over to me all that was truly meaningful to her: her faith and heritage (her father's Swedish Bible) and her life story. As we do this work, we are engaging in a sacred trust that cannot be minimalized. We will learn things about ourselves and each other that may change our perceptions of ourselves, the world and God. Handle with care.

Exercise:

Take time to graph your life story. Where are the highs and lows? Where was God in the midst of those moments? How have those times

served to change or deepen your relationship with God, the church, and others? Where in your present time is God stretching you and calling you to conversion? To begin to understand our hopes and dreams as well as our fears and anxieties extend the graph into the future and repeat the exercise.

If you are using this in Bible Study or as church council discussion material, you might chart the story of the congregation (it is better not to not haul out a history of the congregation but to reconstruct it from what people know and then seek to fill in the gaps from other sources). What are the episodes of the congregation's life that people remember and speak about? What has been forgotten? What is not told? How are recent pastors remembered (both by the congregation and by you). Have there been times that have rocked the congregation? Have there been occasions for great celebration? Where was God in the midst of those moments for the congregation (and for you)? Where is God today? What areas of the life of the congregation are you being called into conversion and new life?

My Story is important not only for what it reveals about me and how I have journeyed with God but it is also the place where we first begin to identify those aspects of our story that will lead to the Front Porches of our faith sharing.

A second exercise I recommend is to take a few moments and develop your "Personal Introduction." By that I mean, if you were to meet someone for the first time and you knew that you wanted to establish a lasting friendship with this person, what three things would it be important for them know about you to really begin to *know* you? I then ask participants to find one other person that they do not know well and each of them share their three things.

I have discovered in paying attention to my relationship building that consistently I reveal pretty quickly in a relationship the following three things about myself: **I am adopted, my father died when I was 13 and that I am a father and grandfather.**

That I am **adopted**. This is a piece of my story that for 62 years was very consistent but with the reuniting of my mom and I is in a major rewrite. My adoption has always been how I have understood myself and my relationship to God and church. When I was in my mid-twenties my mother presented me with my "official papers" which I promptly placed unread in the family safe. It would be years later while searching for one of my kid's birth certificates that my file erupted its contents on the kitchen floor. Suddenly, my adoption and baptismal certificate were before me. In hesitantly examining them I discovered that my adoption was legally finalized on June 26, 1958 (exactly one year from my birth) but I was baptized June 22, 1958 (4 days earlier). It confirmed the truth that I had known for most of my life, God got me first.

While the story of my adoptive family is hardly the stuff for a good Hallmark movie, my experience with being adopted is that it has been a rich blessing. One of the beauties of being adopted is that you can choose your family and you are not limited by normal conventions. I have had over the years dozens of mothers, grandmothers, fathers and grandfathers, brothers and sisters. Each of these relationships have been gift and blessing. While these relationships have been both within and outside of my church families it has been the church that has functioned as my primary family unit. I have always seen myself first and foremost as a child of God.

I have found in sharing this piece of my story that adoption is for many a secret and sometimes embarrassing part of people's stories. It is without exception that after revealing this piece publicly I will have someone come to me during a break to share their adoption story with me (sometimes it is as an adoptee, sometimes it is as a parent/grandparent of an adoptee, sometimes a parent who has put a child up for adoption). These are incredible and powerful encounters. I remember at one gathering a young woman came up to me at break and told me that she had never told anyone that she was adopted. She had come with two of her closest friends and for the first time felt able to share with them her secret. We talked for some time about the feelings she has carried with her that she thought were so abnormal but which in other conversations I have found to be typical adoption feelings. I share this story to show how this single piece of my story has served as a Front Porch from which to establish new and often healing relationships.

I am still processing the latest chapter in my adoption story, that of being reunited with my biological mom. It is already a story of God's grace and love that brought us to this point without either of us really trying but always living in hope that someday it would happen. Stay tuned for the rest of the story.

My **father died** when I was 13. This was an incredibly traumatic chapter of my story because it was clear at least at an unconscious level that it was his desire to adopt and not my mother's. This has, however, been one of the most significant Front Porches in my life. The conversations of death, dying, grief and mourning that have occurred on this porch are innumerable. It was also the porch that I operated from as a hospice chaplain for 15 years.

Finally, that I have **children and grandchildren** (let me show you pictures...). While this may seem like a no-brainer, the kinds of conversations that have developed on this Front Porch are startling. I have had parents and grandparents: tell me of their LGBTQ children/grandchildren, talk about difficulties and struggles they are having with their children/grandchildren, their hopes and dreams for them, the death of children/grandchildren, their children/grandchildren's addictions, their fear that that their children/grandchildren will be raised without faith, their recognition that there will be no grandchildren, I have even had conversations about abortions from this Front Porch. It is a safe porch that can become intimate very easily as we find common ground.

I hope you can see how important knowing and understanding your own faith story is in building and strengthening the Front Porches from which we do the work of sharing our faith both within our congregational families as well as those we encounter outside of them.

Exercise:

What three things about yourself are important for others to know about you if they are to understand you? Share with someone. (Variation: create a Facebook type quiz..." How well do you know_____"? or formulate questions about yourself and invite others to take the quiz).

An exercise that I have used with council's and other gatherings is a group activity where they construct the outline for writing/telling their group story whether it is their council, organization or their congregation.

I have used this to help congregations begin to develop vision statements as well as media materials.

Group Exercise:

Ask the group, if it were to write a story of their life what events would they want to include? What questions might they want answered? What details should be included? Write these on newsprint or a board and then invite the members of the group to begin to address these for themselves as they write the group story. Once the story is developed ask how and to whom is it important to share it with?

CHAPTER 4

GOD'S STORY

That student that I spoke of in the opening of this book who was looking for Jesus highlights the new and important task of telling and telling in new ways, God's story. The new challenge is that we do not have a common scriptural vocabulary. This is true of those we are seeking to reach but it is also true of us within the church. In the 1960's and 70's we replaced Biblical content with an emphasis on values and the curriculum of what's happening now. I do not mean to denigrate those efforts only that what is left is a generation that lacks the grammar for serious telling of God's story. In my work in developing the adult catechumenate model of evangelization in the church I created what I believe a first step in reclaiming this grammar. I call it "Sacred Syntax". I believe if we all know and can tell these 50 some stories from scripture we will have a common language of symbols, images and stories to address in a coherent way the story of God and God's people. These form the syntax of biblical conversation:

Sacred Syntax

1. Creation (Genesis 1:1—2:4a and 2:4b-25)
2. The fall (Genesis 3)
3. Cain and Abel (Genesis 4:1-16)
4. Noah (Genesis 6:5—9:28)
5. Babel (Genesis 11:1-9)

6. Call of Abram (Genesis 11:31—12:6)
7. Covenant with Abraham (Genesis 15)
8. Joseph (Genesis 37–45)
9. Burning bush (Exodus 3)
10. Passover (Exodus 11:1—12:36)
11. Crossing of the Red Sea (Exodus 13:17—15:21)
12. Ten Commandments (Exodus 20:1-17; Deuteronomy 5:6-21)
13. Golden calf (Exodus 32)
14. Great Commandment (Deuteronomy 6:4-9)
15. Samson (Judges 13–16)
16. Goliath (1 Samuel 17)
17. David and Bathsheba (2 Samuel 11:1—12:25)
18. Elijah meets God (1 Kings 19:1-13)
19. Job (Job 1:13-22)
20. Psalm 23
21. Call of Jeremiah (Jeremiah 1:1-10)
22. Infancy narratives (Matthew 1:1—2:23; Luke 1:1—2:52)
23. Temptation of Jesus (Matthew 4:1-11; Mark 1:12-13; Luke 4:1-13)
24. Beatitudes (Matthew 5:1-11; Luke 6:20-23)
25. Lord's Prayer (Matthew 6:5-14; Luke 11:2-4)
26. Sower and seeds (Matthew 13:1-9, 18-23; Mark 4:1-9; Luke 8:4-8)
27. Good Samaritan (Luke 10:25-37)
28. Mary and Martha (Luke 10:38-42)
29. Prodigal son (Luke 15:11-32)
30. Lazarus and the rich man (Luke 16:19-31)
31. Zacchaeus (Luke 19:1-10)
32. Wedding at Cana (John 2:1-12)
33. Woman at the well (John 4:3-42)
34. Bread of life (John 6)
35. Woman caught in adultery (John 7:53—8:11)
36. Man born blind (John 9:1-41)
37. Good shepherd (John 10)
38. Raising of Lazarus (John 11:1-44)
39. Feeding of the multitudes (Matthew 14:13-21; Mark 6:30-44; Luke 9:10-17; John 6:1-14)

40. Prediction of Jesus' death (Matthew 16:21-28; Mark 8:31—9:1; Luke 9:21-27)
41. Lost sheep (Matthew 18:10-14; Luke 15:3-7)
42. Great Commandment, New Testament version (Matthew 22:34-40; Mark 12:28-34; Luke 10:25-28)
43. Final judgment (Matthew 25:31-46)
44. Passion (Matthew 26–27; Mark 14–15; Luke 22–23; John 13–19)
45. Lord's Supper (Matthew 26:26-30; Mark 14:22-26; Luke 22:14-23; 1 Corinthians 11:23-26)
46. Resurrection (Matthew 28:1-15; Mark 16:1-8; Luke 24:1-12; John 20:1-10)
47. Emmaus (Luke 24:13-35)
48. Thomas (John 20:24-29)
49. Jesus appears to the disciples/Ascension (Matthew 28:16-20; Luke 24:36-50; John 20:19-23; Acts 1:6-11)
50. Pentecost (Acts 2:1-13)
51. Stoning of Stephen (Acts 6:8—8:2)
52. Conversion of Paul (Acts 9:1-30)
53. Grace (Romans 1–3)

This list is not meant to be exhaustive but rather a starting point.

One of my pet peeves is that in this church whenever we advocate reading the Bible, we put another book in between the Bible and ourselves. Before we can read the Bible, we seem to have to construct a hermeneutic and a style of study. I believe that before we can have *those* discussions it would be helpful if we know the book of which we speak. I advocate that we cannot use the above stories enough in the life of our congregations. Use them as personal devotions, open meetings with a dwelling in them, I have gone so far as to develop Sunday School curriculum around them… the possibilities are endless, and the results are crucial if we are indeed serious about our call to share the story with others.

That said, those that gather on our Front Porches both from the street as well as those that regularly gather together with us as church need assistance dealing with material that is 2000 years or better removed from them. To that end I developed a simple introduction to scripture, **Holy Talk: An Introduction to Scripture for the Occasionally Biblically**

Embarrassed (LuLu Press) that can serve as a model for Bible Study or such opportunities as Dwelling in the Word. My hope is that this offers a new way of approaching scripture that leads us to a direct encounter with the God that calls and gathers us in the Spirit.

A second difficulty for many of us in the church in appropriating the Scriptures into daily life is the fact that we rarely deal with the Bible as a whole or in overview. Instead we encounter it piecemeal in Sunday morning periscopes or by book in Bible Study. What follows is intended as a brief overview that can serve as a framework for our ongoing encounter with the Bible. As such I will not be utilizing the common Old/New Testament demarcations.

Where do we begin? Surprisingly, not with Genesis or Matthew. Instead we begin with the historical event of the Exile. The year - 580 BCE.

Babylon (Iraq) has just kicked the backside of God's people, destroyed Jerusalem and the Temple, and taken as POW's the cream of the crop of God's people...anyone who might be able to organize a revolt or resistance to Babylon's occupation. This produces a crisis of epic proportions. Suddenly, all that God's people have held as sacred and invaluable is left in ashes and ruble.

Their prior existence as God's people was built around three promises from God:

- Promised Land
- Promised Temple worship
- Promised king like David forever

All of these are taken away and God's people find themselves in a full-blown faith crisis.

- Who is our God? Is there God?
- Who are we without our promises?
- How do we live in community together here in Babylon?
- What does God want us to do with our lives?
- And as time goes on...Will our children have faith?

In the midst of their anxiety and fear they begin to ask the question: When have we found ourselves in a situation like this before? Their answer: in the Exodus. *(As economic crisis grips the present-day United States, I find my older friends remembering and rehearsing the Great Depression in much the same way)*. It too was a time when existence was at the mercy of the arbitrary power of the Pharaoh of Egypt. This too was a helpless and hopeless situation. God intervenes by sending his "champion", Moses. In so doing God accomplishes a three-fold outcome: Deliverance from the bondage of the Pharaoh, the establishment of Covenant (I will be your God and you will be my people), and the giving of the Law (This is how I expect my people to live together). The story of the Exodus becomes the defining story in Israel's history: God's people find themselves in a hopeless/helpless situation usually at the hands of a foreign power-broker (one also often characterized by a failure of God's people to keep covenant with God and with each other) ...God intervenes...God reestablishes the broken relationship.

While God's people find themselves sitting by the Tigris and Euphrates, dangling their footsies in the river and reflecting on the Exodus they begin to formulate questions about their current situation. The first of those is, "How did we get in this mess in the first place?" Their answer (as we find it in their historical books: 1 & 2 Samuel and 1 & 2 Kings *et al)* is, that it's all been downhill since we got a king. In addition to the historical recital that we find here the prophets also weighed in on the situation both prior to the Exile and during it. There is a call to recommit to the keeping of the Torah/Law. The prophets' message is both a note of judgment and hope. One of the sources of that hope is the promise of a deliverer/Messiah (like Moses) who will enable God's people to return to the promised land. That promise is fulfilled when Cyrus, King of Persia (and newest bully on the block), sweeps in, defeats Babylon, and sets God's people free to return home.

Rather than the mass exodus of a previous generation this return to the Promised Land was carried out by a relatively few of the exiles. Upon returning home they found their situation pretty desperate...and it only gets worse. Before long Alexander and his Greek fraternity sweep in and again reduce God's people to a vassal people. In time they are replaced by Caesar and his cohorts. Caesar and the Romans are invited in to assist in riding Judah of the Greeks. Surprise, surprise, they not only expel the Greeks, but they set up shop in the region as an occupation army. With each new wave of "occupiers" comes renewed resistance (often violent) and a renewed reflection which leads to the development and speculation concerning the coming of a Messiah. This Messiah was to be a great military leader that would kick the invaders back home and reestablish the Glory Days of Israel or he would be a religious leader who would reestablish right worship of God, or a combination of both. It is into this speculative situation that Jesus of Nazareth is born.

The earliest "Christian" writings in scripture are not the gospels but rather writings of Paul. One can hardly construct a biographical narrative of Jesus from the works of Paul. Paul is far more interested in supporting the budding congregations of early Christianity in the midst of their "crises" and divisive tendencies. In many ways Paul functions like a modern bishop or "firefighter".

It is not until around the later part of the first century that we find the new literary genre we know as the gospels. The gospels are not biographies in the modern sense of the word but are rather theological reflections on the life, death and resurrection of Jesus. Mark is the evangelical gospel. Mark calls us into the story of Jesus and sends us out with that same story to share with others. With Matthew and Luke, the church is developing the catechetical/teaching materials that are needed: Matthew is the curriculum for Jewish converts (Jesus is portrayed as the new Moses) and Luke for those non-Jews (where Jesus has a heroic flavor like those of Greek mythology). John's gospel is our gospel – the church's gospel. John is writing to insiders who gather for worship regularly. As a result, John had little need to remind to a people who attend the Eucharist about the institution of the Last Supper, but he does need to remind us about how we who gather at that meal are sent to serve (foot washing). John's intent is to call the church to continued faithfulness through the crucified and risen Christ with Abba/Daddy God.

There are several pieces of biblical material that I have not touched on, first, the material in Genesis. While in Babylon God's people were redefining their identity beyond that of a particular people dedicated to a particular piece of land. Genesis is a cosmic rehearsal and collection of the stories of the past that point to the cosmic nature of God and God's extensive relationship with them that even predates their being called out of Egypt. It is not all that unlike some of the foundational stories of our own nation: Daniel Boone, Davey Crockett, Paul Bunyan, John Henry and Joe Magarac.

There is also the Wisdom literature (sic. Psalms, Proverbs, Ecclesiastes). This material is an attempt to push the boundaries of faith beyond the confines of Temple and synagogue and into the streets. It is practical theology. In modern times there is a resurgence of this type in much of the "New Age" materials.

Finally, there is the apocalyptic material of books like Daniel and the Revelation of St. John. These are perhaps the most misused books of all of scripture. Rather than timetables for gloom and doom they are meant as books of hope. Apocalyptic literature in general appears in times of crises. It is an attempt in the midst of uncertainty and terror to remind us of how the story is going to turn out. If we know that in the end all will be in God's hands, we are enabled to live with hope and confidence even in the midst of terror *(When in college I was dragged by friends to my one and only experience of a horror flick. I left after 30 minutes. For six months I slept with the lights on and music playing. What I realize now is that I did not know how the story ended and so the terror persisted).* "I am the Alpha and the Omega, the beginning and the end..." God's got this one under control we can live securely as God's people regardless of what we may encounter.

Exercises:

1. *Pick one of the stories from the list of Sacred Syntax. Make a point to read it daily for a week. At the end of the week find someone to tell the story to and in your own words share the story with them. I have the Bible on CD so I will pick a story and play it in the car for a week every time I go somewhere. Repeat this exercise periodically until you work your way through the list.*

2. *Form groups of about 6-8 people.*

   • *Without opening the Bible. Establish your version of the story. Characters, plot, location*

- *When you have established your story ask the question: what do I know about this story? What other Biblical stories might be related? Do you remember what is going on around the story? What does the story say about: God? Me/Us? Living in Community?*

3. *Several congregations have used this as a year-round exercise. In an adult class or other group they work with one story each week over the course of a year. They use the following questions as the jumping off place for their discussions:*

What does the story say about...?

- *Who God is?*
- *Who we are as God's people?*
- *How do we live in community together?*
- *What does God want us to do with our lives?*
- *And as time goes on...Will our children have faith?*

CHAPTER 5

MY STORY/GOD'S STORY

Regardless of the methodology there is always a tendency to make the Bible a head trip. Regardless of our starting point and our best intentions we fall prey to talking *about* the Bible, *about* God, and *about* Jesus. Frankly, it's safer that way. To allow Scripture to become a matter of the heart is to open ourselves and the world to be transformed – under no circumstances should that be taken lightly!

Yet if it does not become a matter of the heart it will remain words on a page. The miracle of the Christ event is the incarnation…the Word become flesh. It is that enfleshed Word that we are called to bear to the world. As with the Greeks who came to Phillip, those who come to us come not to find out about Jesus but to encounter Jesus in the flesh and it is the earthen vessel of our flesh that Jesus has chosen to take on. It is not a matter of getting the Scripture into our hearts but seeing the Christ who already abides there. We are but sacraments, blessed and broken, that reveal the one who dwells among us full of grace and truth.

How do we come to know this Christ who dwells in, with and under us? In the early church it was called breaking open the Word. It was the activity of the catechumenate as they gathered in preparation for baptism. They would gather around the texts that they had just heard in worship with questions very similar to those we used in the last chapter: What does this word have to say about: Who is God? Who am I? How do we live in community together? What does God want us to do with our lives?

The issue becomes for us, what does this word have to say about our lives of faith? Where does God's story meet My Story? We need to reach the point where we begin to do this questioning every time we hear scripture shared whether it is on Sunday morning in worship, in our homes for devotion, when we gather for Bible Study, or when we read scripture at the beginning of a meeting. This does not happen overnight nor does it happen without some intentionality.

I believe the best approach is multifaceted and saturated. Do it whenever and wherever to opportunity arises.

- Don't wait for the pastor to tell you what the readings for Sunday morning mean. Read the texts prior to Sunday (if your church does not provide a listing of the next Sunday's readings ask for them to be provided). Sit with those readings and your questions. You will be amazed at what you begin to hear in those sermons.

- Instead of being satisfied with those little reflections on the readings that so many devotionals provide, sit with the daily reading(s) and your questions.

- Use the questions as the structure for your Bible Study instead of turning to the "resident expert" (whether in body or print) to illuminate the text.

- As you begin council or committee meetings use the coming Sunday's gospel reading and the questions to prepare yourselves to do the work that is before you. It might be helpful that before you begin the process you might identify the issues before you in that meeting (i.e. As we begin our devotions tonight let us remember that we will be dealing with matters of worship planning or budget or faith formation, etc.…).

- Start small group gatherings in your homes, coffee houses, restaurants with multigenerational gatherings around Scripture and these questions.

This process of internalizing the word done in this way accomplished two outcomes. First, we take and eat that Word that comes to us sweeter than honey and secondly, we begin to become more comfortable talking about scripture and our faith with others. If we become more comfortable talking about these things with those we know how much easier will it be when we find ourselves in situations with those we do not know as well?

Exercise 1

- *Read story of Mary and Martha (Luke 10:38-42) (or chose a story for Sacred Syntax) outloud 2x's with different voices (Male/Female). Pay attention to the words or phrases that catch your attention (you may wish to jot them down).*
- *Prayerfully reflect on what you heard in the story. Begin with the words that caught your attention. This is where God is speaking to you at this moment.*
- *Reflect on the 3 Questions: What does the story say about: God? Me/Us? Living in Community? And a 4ᵗʰ question: What is God saying to me? What is being asked of me?*

Exercise 2 A man had two sons.... Prodigal Son (Exiled Son)

- *Tell story. Pay attention to the three main characters in the story. Who captures your attention most TODAY? Stay with that character as you listen to the story.*
- *Who caught your attention? Break up into groups Younger Son, Older Son, Father. Discuss what about that character resonated with you today?*
- *IN THE LARGE GROUP SPLIT UP INTO GROUPS OF NO MORE THAN 4.* What does the story say about: God? Me/Us? Living in Community? And a 4ᵗʰ question: What is God saying to me? What is being asked of me?
- *What was it like? Commonality? Did you hear the story from a different reference point that normal today?*

The story of the Prodigal Son has become a foundational story for me in telling my faith journey. I am an oldest son (with a brother just like the youngest). As such I found the story quite unfair. I even went so far as to create an Older Son version of the story where the father comes out, takes the older son by the arm, leads him into the banquet hall, kicks his younger brother out of the guest of honor chair and sits the older son in his rightful position as guest of honor and favored son. That was my point of reference until I had my first child, who insisted on living out the life of the youngest son. Then I learned about what it meant to be the Father. No matter what he did I would continue to welcome him back with open arms (maybe not with robe and ring). Until several years ago I had no understanding or sympathy for the prodigal. It was when I did a Lenten series on Henri Nouwen's, **Return of the Prodigal** that I realized that I too was an exiled son.

As I mentioned earlier, my father's death was a decisive chapter in my life. I came out of that event shaken in my faith. If Billy Joel was right, and only the good die young, then I no longer wished to be good. I didn't have to figure out how to be bad because my mother had been telling me all my life, "Stay away from the Smith boys because they are bad." So, I searched them out. For the better part of two years I followed their lead (but by the grace of God I did not end up in jail or dead, for both were possible outcomes). For those years I lived a double life: the good son by day and the bad son by night.

While I didn't have a pig sty moment, I eventually realized this was simply not who I was. It was then that the real crisis began for me: When I would go home my father would not be there with robe, or ring or fatted calf… he would not be there at all!

It was then I embarked on a journey to find a new home. Perhaps academics could be my new home? I threw myself into my studies and became the model student. But academics was not my home. I thought music could be home, but it too was not home. I tried countless relationships which all ended disastrously, there was no home there either. I would become a pastor and find a congregation to be my home – didn't happen. I'd get married and start a family; they would be my home… wrong! In desperation I decided that if I could find Jesus, I would find my home. I searched and searched. I practiced and devoted, engaged in theological speculation and pious life but still I could not find Jesus or home. Then one day God showed up on the road with robe and ring and fatted calf. Arms outstretched he picked me up in the midst of my stammering confession and simply said, welcome home.

CHAPTER 6

MY STORY/YOUR STORY

I am sure that we have had the experience of watching a commercial on the television and wondered who they were aiming at because it was obviously not us. There is intense research behind the decisions of what commercial to run when and with what shows. Much of what passes for evangelism these days tries the same "targeted" approach. Who is your audience…millennials? X-ers? Young adults? (note rarely does anyone ever target the over 50 crowd or the outcast). Such an approach is not only dehumanizing it is unbiblical. Jesus didn't have a target audience but rather responded to those who his Father placed in his path. So too with us. We rarely have to go looking for encounters…God has a way of laying them at our feet (on any given day we might gladly wish that God would lay these persons at someone else's feet). They are coworkers, family members (often in-laws), students, teachers, they are those we share coffee with, those who wait on us, those who sit next to us on the plane, those sharing a waiting room…the list is endless…God's target is indeed the whole world!

When I was young my mother used to introduce me, "This is my son, Harold, Oh, he's shy." For years I used to think that the "O" in my name stood for "O, he's shy." I simply assumed that I was shy. It was quite convenient. There are things shy kids do like read books and take music lessons and there are things that shy kids don't do like play sports or volunteer for parts in plays. While pursuing my clinical studies I picked up a book one day from the hospital chaplain's library entitled, **Shyness.** What I discovered was that I was not shy after all, but I was socially challenged.

This condition has led to an intentional and at times painful and awkward rehabilitation. The first thing I discovered was that God had indeed blessed me with the gifts necessary to begin with – two ears. As we seek to build relationships with those God has graced our lives with, we begin by listening. That is easier said than done because we are not taught to really listen well these days.

For the past decade I have been resourcing a domestic violence agency on the art of active/reflective listening. Reflective listening is a special type of listening that involves paying respectful attention to the content and feelings of another's communication, hearing and understanding; and then letting the other know that he or she is being heard and understood. It is a two-step process that calls us to 1) hear and understand what the other is saying through words and non-verbal communication; 2) reflect (express) the thoughts and feeling you heard through your own words, tone of voice, posture and gestures so that the other knows that he or she is heard and understood.

A high premium is placed on being "heard" today probably because it happens so rarely in our culture. The church specifically has languished under the perception (accurate or not) that it is no longer listening to the people/world. If we are to have any significant outcomes with our efforts to share our faith then we must establish relationships in which there is an element not only of trust but also the sense of having their needs, wants, desires, fears, etc…, be "heard".

Some of the skills that are utilized in this reflective listening are:

- **Feedback:** A response that acknowledges what you heard the other say.
- **Questions:** Clarification questions only! (i.e. " I am not sure I got this point you were making, are you saying….?" or "I am confused, are we still talking about your experiences in this church or another?").
- **Paraphrasing:** This will be awkward at first but the more you practice the easier it gets. Repeat back to them in your own words

what you think you heard. (i.e. "Let me be sure I have this right, are you saying…").

- **Confrontation:** A relationship needs to be very developed before this can be used successfully. I find it most useful when getting conflicting communications. In a case where the person insists that they are at ease with a certain topic and yet their body language speaks of holding it in tightly I might say something like, "I hear what you are saying but you look uncomfortable with this issue." Other times it might be conflicting statements and I might challenge with a question for clarification, "You have said 'x' and 'y', which is it that you intended?"

In my work with domestic violence victims I have discovered that there are serious roadblocks to the building of this trust and "hearing". I have encountered many of these in efforts to "evangelize" me as well as debriefing those who have been "evangelized". These include comments that are:

- **Probing or Questioning:** "Inquiring minds want to know" often more than we need to know or that others wish to share. Questions should always be only for clarifying things that we are unsure of in the conversation.
- **Criticizing or Name-Calling:** Most of us would not intentionally engage in this kind of behavior and yet it is easy to subtly slide into it. Calling into question the way another is putting together their faith or beliefs that they might hold says that you are more interested in preserving your faith system than in hearing their struggles. For example, I have a friend that occasionally consults a medium. The first time he mentioned it I internally recoiled. What I have discovered because I did not cut the conversation off by criticizing his choice was that his experiences with this medium for him are very similar to what I have encountered well-respected therapists doing with clients. The name-calling can be even more subtle. Labels often are a "polite" form of name-calling: unbeliever, seeker, un-churched are used regularly in evangelism "speak" and yet their nature categorizes and judges those they label.

- **Sarcasm:** It requires a fairly sophisticated understanding to decipher sarcasm. Our ability is greatly impaired when in stress or dealing with emotional issues.

- **Interpreting/Analyzing:** As we are building relationships our task is not to try to "figure the other person out" but rather to hear what they are sharing.

- **Moralizing/Ordering/Threatening:** These are often tactics that many have encountered when engaged by "evangelists". I have discovered that even getting close to these with someone who has experienced an "evangelist" or church using them is enough to send them running. Such statements as, "If you do not wish to spend eternity in hell then you must accept Jesus as personal Lord and Savior" are sure-fire ways of ending a relationship.

- **Arguing/Lecturing/Persuading:** Remember as you begin working on a relationship you are being invited in to listen...do not abuse that. It is not your agenda that is important but the Holy Spirit's – don't confuse them.

- **Sympathizing/Reassuring/Excusing:** While these seem noble responses they can easily become a message that says that it's ok for them to stay where they are in their journey. The work of the Holy Spirit is always transforming us...we don't need to try to help by closing doors on such opportunity.

My former colleague, Pastor Neil Harrison, would regularly remind staff that our work as evangelists was about "Relationship, relationship, relationship: Relationship with Jesus and with one another." Until we are in relationship with the other it is very difficult to talk about deep matters of faith and life. To build these relationships takes time.

Joe, who was emotionally/mentally challenged, came to live with his brother after their father died. His brother informed him, in my presence, that if he every wanted to go to church he should go to mine (how his brother could come to that conclusion having never been there himself was beyond me). This began a long-standing relationship and daily conversation that went like this:

Hi, Pastor Jake!
Hi, Joe! How are you doing?
I'm fine. How about you Pastor Jake?
I'm good.
How's the church?
The church is doing well.
(end of conversation)

This went on for the better part of a year when I had one of those days and decided to have some fun with Joe by changing the conversation:

Hi, Pastor Jake!
Hi, Joe! How are you doing?
I'm fine. How about you Pastor Jake?
I'm good.
How's the church?
The church is doing well. I have a seat saved for you.
Ha, ha, ha… that's a funny one!
(end of conversation)

Again, a year passed when one day the conversation went like this:

Hi, Pastor Jake!
Hi, Joe! How are you doing?
I'm fine. How about you Pastor Jake?
I'm good.
How's the church?
The church is doing well. I have a seat saved for you.
Ha, ha, ha… that's a funny one! What time is church?
11:00.

Joe was there and never missed a Sunday until he had to go to a facility when he could no longer manage his medications.

I share this because you never know at what stage of the journey together the conversation will suddenly go deeper. We need to be ready for God's time… that's why our Front Porchin' work is important.

Exercises:

1. *Pair with a partner. One will be the listener the other the speaker. If you are the listener you cannot speak, only listen. For about 5 minutes the speaker will talk (I usually suggest a holiday or season coming up as content: How will you celebrate Christmas? What will/did you do/did on vacation?). reverse roles.*

2. *Find someone you do not know well. Have a normal unstructured conversation. When you find a common touchstone in the conversation spend the remaining time talking about it. What did you learn? How long before you found a common story. These are the Front Porches of our relationship where we find that common ground to build on.*

3. *Take some time to remember a pleasant or exciting time/event in your life. Try to remember as many details as possible. Share this memory with a partner (pay particular attention to how it feels to share this with another and how you feel that you are being heard). Partner, remember that your task is to listen. Questions should be for clarification only. Focus of what it feels like to listen. Switch roles. When both have shared talk about your experiences and listener and hearer. What did you feel? Which was harder, listening or speaking? How did you feel received by the one listening.*

4. *Repeat exercise #3 using a difficult situation or tough time in your life.*

5. *I have found a very helpful exercise to use with all ages that begins to reach the emotional level that often develops when we talk about faith issues is this:*

Ask participants to close their eyes and remember back to a September day...this particular September day had a great impact on many of our lives...the day is September 11, 2001...(allow time for it to sink in before continuing)...remember where you were when you first heard or saw the news...What are the sights, words, sounds, images that come to mind? What did you find yourself doing? How did you feel? (allow them some time to dwell in these)

Now I would ask you to partner with another and share your memories of that day. Remember you will each have an opportunity to speak so when you are the listener – LISTEN! Pay particular attention to your own emotions/reactions as both listener and speaker.

Allow 15 minutes for this (You will have to break off the discussion). Debrief what has occurred. How did it feel as listener? speaker? Were you heard? Did you have difficulty reflectively listening?

A particularly powerful moment happened at one of these sessions. Following the Listener/Speaker exercise (#1) an older woman came up to me in tears and said, "Thank you, no one has ever listened to me before."

What we experience in encounters like this is the mystery of the incarnation. Jesus reminds us, "Where two or three gather in my name, I am there with them." Whenever we engage another in this way we enter into a sacred moment, holy time.

As I shared earlier, my life story has taken a dramatic turn in recent months as my biological mother and I have been reunited. When we tell the story of our reunion it almost always brings tears to those who hear it. This has mystified both my mom and me. Recently I shared the story with a group of very close friends, and it produced the now predictable strong emotional response. Because we were close, I asked if they knew why they were reacting in such a manner.

One of them said because we hear that story through our own stories. In her case it was a contrast between the love that I had found and the love that she never knew. We view the world through our stories (whether we recognize it or not). It is why this process of getting to know each other's stories is so important. It impacts how we chose to share that story as well as what clues to listen to from those who are listening.

CHAPTER 7

MY STORY/YOUR STORY/ GOD'S STORY

As I mentioned earlier every encounter with another is a sacred moment and every such encounter brings with it the mystery of the incarnate Jesus, therefore, we do not have to *bring* Jesus into the relationship – he's already there. Our task then is to point to the already existent presence of Christ. What we are essentially talking about is faith – perceiving what God already promises to be true.

I like to use an old Sufi story to illustrate. Nasirdim was a world-famous smuggler, Everyone knew he was a smuggler they just couldn't catch him at it. Some days he would go down to the border and the border guards would strip him of his clothes, take all the bags off of his donkeys but in the end they never found anything suspicious.

Nasirdim retires at age 30 a wealthy man and decides to throw a party for the border guards. After a few drinks one of the guards becomes emboldened enough to ask, "Nasirdim, we know that you are a smuggler and yet we could never catch you. Now that you're retiring what was it that you were smuggling?" Nasirdim paused and then disclosed, "Donkeys."

It is not that Jesus is absent from people's lives it is rather that we don't perceive his presence. Our task as evangelists is to show the world Jesus. We do that incarnationally...we are embodied witnesses. Sometimes our challenge is to identify the Jesus that is already at work in the world.

One of the execises I like to do with leadership teams is to ask them where they have seen Jesus in the last 48 hours. After they get past the deer in the headlight look and realize that I expect them to answer the question, they usually are able to begin to identify the work of Jesus in their world. One particular group I worked with for about a year got very good at that identifying. When I spoke to them about how much they had grown with the exercise, one woman responded, "It's easier to see Jesus when you are looking for him!" Yes!

In my work as a spiritual director I have found myself better able to recognize the Spirit's movement in a person's life. This does not happen magically or overnight. For me it has come as I have learned to seek to discover the presence of that Spirit working in my life. That is why the piece My Story/God's Story is so critical to effective evangelism. That piece also needs to remain a continuing discipline. It is only when we begin to recognize the murmurings and stirrings of the Spirit in our own lives that we can begin to recognize them in the lives of those who end up on our front porch.

A second learning from my work as a spiritual director is that my task is not to *take* them *somewhere* (even if I believe I know where they need to go). My call is to walk with them. It is to listen to them and to God/Spirit in the midst of that journey helping them to see and to recognize the presence and movement of God in that journey. We are called to be sacramental pilgrim listeners. Sacramental in the sense that we point/reveal one who is beyond us. Pilgrim in that we journey *with* them. Listeners in that our primary function is to listen to both them and God in a way that we might be faithful sacraments revealing the presence of God to the other.

I have also found that the more I dwell in my own spiritual journey (My Story/God's Story) to the point of being better able to see God acting in my life and the more I dwell in God's Story (immersing myself in God's syntax) the easier and more natural I am able to bring those two elements to bear upon my encounters with the Your Story piece.

Exercise:

(Individual) Refer back to your timeline. Pick an event or a stage of your life. Where was God in the midst of that event/time? Can

you identify biblical stories (see Sacred Syntax) or themes (grace, forgiveness, redemption) that are similar to that time?

(Group) Chose an experience (I have found that using one from the previous section often works well). Talk about how God was present in that situation (feeling that God was absent in particular situations is perfectly acceptable). Following the presentation to the group. Invite the group then to provide Biblical stories, personalities, themes or images that this presentation surfaced for them. (This will be difficult at first but be persistent).

CHAPTER 8

WHERE DO WE GO
FROM HERE

In the first seven chapters of this book I have laid out a process of faith sharing that is designed to work within the life of the congregation. As we seek ways of composing and sharing our faith stories among people with which we already have a common story we will find it easier when needing to share that story outside of the congregational setting.

I encourage you to create opportunities throughout the year to do faith sharing in meaningful ways. This may be in small group settings, one on one's, council or committee meetings.

The poster congregation for Front Porchin' is Faith Evangelical Lutheran Church in White Oak, PA, a small mill town outside of Pittsburgh. They chose to implement the process through a Bible study model. They began with a small group gathered around the Sacred Syntax stories Bible studies. They started by using the method of encountering scripture outlined in chapters 3 and 4. Finding themselves at the end of the list after a year they realized their work was not done. They created their own list of parables for the second year of encounter. They are now on year three and gather 20-30 people every Tuesday morning. I was recently able to join them for some "testimony" on their experiences. It was a powerful gathering as the group shared their faith stories and their journey together over the past three years. They spoke of it not only transforming their lives but also the life of the congregation.

This is but one way to root the Front Porchin' process into the life of the congregation. Others have used conversation starters at church dinners such as: "Who first taught you about Jesus?" "Who were exemplars of faith in your life?" "What are your favorite memories of church as a child?" "What is your favorite part of worship?" Other congregations have established the practice of beginning council meetings with the question: "Where have you seen Jesus this past month?" Still others have begun including Faith Sharing Moments as part of their announcements before worship.

CHAPTER 9

NEXT STEPS (OR FRONT PORCHIN' 102)

For the last several years I have been getting requests to provide additional materials. As I began that process, I was surprised that the Front Porchin' process itself drove my thoughts.

Several years ago, I was having breakfast with my good friend and Baptist colleague, Keith Richardson. We were discussing the future of the church. He shared with me that he had been discerning in his prayers that if the Baptists were to have a future in this rapidly changing world that they would have to learn grace. He went on to say that the Baptists don't do grace well but that we as Lutherans do and have an obligation to the church to faithfully teach and practice that grace.

In the world we are living in, both secular and religious, grace is a very unpopular word. I believe that without grace we will continue down the dark path we have been on for decades both as church and society.

We have been given a great opportunity to lead the church boldly into the future. What we over the next several years will have an impact on the whole church and the communities we live in as well. I will not sugar coat it – it will be hard work. It will take the best that each one of us has to offer to the effort if we are to succeed.

I feel like I have been stumbling in the dark these past few years in trying to lead the church into the future. A light is beginning to dawn. I am beginning to understand better what kind of leadership (the more the merrier) it will take to keep pace with the speed with which the world is changing. I also feel like I've just been hit over the head with a heavenly *graceball* bat. Grace is what transforms us, the baptized, on a daily basis so why was it so hard to realize that it will be grace that will transform us as the church and the world.

As I have been working on a follow-up to my work on faith sharing, *Front Porchin'* I have identified three general loci for God's transforming grace: ourselves/Home; the gathered body/Church and the neighbor/World. I will focus our discussions and our future programming around those three loci. Part 2 will use these 3 loci to expand the Front Porchin' into a sense of Transforming Grace.

NOTE: A down-loadable version of the Front Porchin' workbook is available by contacting the author @ jakejacobson77@gmail.com.

PART 2
TRANSFORMING GRACE

OVERVIEW

As I look at the implementation of Front Porchin' (FP) in the life of a congregation I have located three loci of activity (home, church, community) within the larger context of the three stories (My Story, God's Story, Our Story). If we are looking at transformative grace emanating from the work of Front Porchin' then these three loci are the places where that grace needs to be nurtured and tended. The work of transformation is the work of the Holy Spirit, but we open and nurture the space for the Spirit to work.

It is important to recognize that the transformation process operates in all three areas but may proceed at different rates. I personally may experience transformation in my life before the congregation reaches the same level of transformation. This can be frustrating for both the congregation and the individual. Careful monitoring of this is a necessity so that the frustration does not become debilitating for the process.

MY STORY

Our transformative journey in grace always begins where we are. We begin with **My story**, whether we do that as an individual, as a congregation or as the community we are called to serve. Who are we? What is God up to in our lives?

Home

One of the startling discoveries that I have encountered in my work with FP is the level of unreflective living we do. Our society encourages us to be reactive (we are more easily controlled and manipulated that way). The reflective life has always been a hallmark of Christianity but has been too often relegated to the cloister and religious orders.

To seek transformation or conversion in our lives we must be attentive to how God is stirring our lives on a daily basis. One of the simple forms of such reflection is to take 5-10 minutes either at the end or the beginning of the day and review the past 24 hours with the question, "Where was God in all of this?" in mind.

A more structured form of review that I have adapted from Ignatian Spirituality uses these questions:

This day...

- What am I most grateful for?
- What do I want for myself?
- In what ways have I experienced God's love?
- What choices have been inadequate responses to God's love?
- How will I let God lead me into a brighter tomorrow?

Whatever instrument you chose to use the important thing is consistent reflection on our daily life. Each day is a new page in our story. It is from that story that we take the insights to better understand ourselves and the world around us.

Church

How do we story our life together in the gathered congregation?

The first question to pose is, "Is this reflective storying happening already in the congregation and where?" One of the informal ways I have observed this in congregations is in the informal gathering before worship, meetings or other gatherings. What I call "checking in" with one another is storying the congregation. It is collecting the individual experiences into a larger context. This is extremely important work for a congregation to do. A congregation that does this well usually has a handle on the individual stories that make up the congregational family as well as weaving them into a larger story of how God is moving within the congregation's life.

The question I am asking these days is, "Are there ways to formally or more intentionally do this work?" I am not advocating anything that diminishes the informal sharing but simply offering a more intentional way of sharing life together.

One of those places is in the announcements. In recent years I have observed the repurposing of this time in many congregations. It can be a time to share announcements, prayer concerns, updates and milestones (birthdays, anniversaries, births, new jobs.... etc.). In my very brief stint as a Rotarian I experienced what they called "Happy Dollars" which for a dollar donation you could share good news with the group. What if we had Grace-moments instead where people could have the opportunity to share how God has been at work in their lives recently.

Another area I have been utilizing is meeting times. Using 10 minutes to check in with members of a committee or council and then at the end asking if there are concerns or individuals that we need to include in our closing prayer. I have found in this a wealth of connectiveness. In those settings concern for friends and neighbors seem to surface in a different way than in the worship setting.

As I have worked on this project, I am realizing that pastoral visitation in all forms is also a storying process. Intentionally helping individuals to share parts of their story as it relates to the congregation's story is helpful and is also a great source of material to fill the story out or to check out gaps and inconsistencies.

A final, formal way of helping the congregation story its life is a series of questions I use for planning which I adapted from ***Canoeing the Mountains*** (Tod Bolsinger). What is our DNA? What are the things we do in this place that if we ceased to do them, we would cease to be us? Another question I have used to come at the story from an outside perspective is to ask, "If this congregation ceased to exist tomorrow what would the community miss or be lacking?"

Neighbor

Where do we have inroads into the community already?

Where does the congregation's story intersect with the community's story? How does that intersection shape both stories? For example, in my community I have served as: Little League Coach, YMCA Basketball

Coach, a member of the board of several non-profit corporations, a singer in the university and community choirs, a band booster and several more roles. In each of these I was shaped by my interaction with the community and vice versa. The same applies for the church that hosts Alcoholics Anonymous meetings, Boy and Girl Scouts, works with the local domestic violence agency, provides dinners for the hungry, staffs a food bank, etc. A wonderful exercise I have developed is to ask a gathering of the congregation where the congregation already impacts the community. I usually start a list on newsprint. I then ask the individuals gathered to write down where their lives regularly intersect with the public sphere. I then add those lists to the congregational list. The results can be very informative and helpful. I did this with a gathering of about 25 people and in 20 minutes they determined that they had well over 100 Front Porches already reaching into the community from which they were able to share their faith.

We should actively reflect on what we are learning about the community and ourselves from those interactions. How is our ministry being shaped and informed by the outreach into the community? What new pieces of the community's story are we learning? How will these learnings help us in future outreach endeavors? What are we doing well? What is in need of overhaul? What programs have reached the end of their effectiveness?

All too often this kind of assessment of outreach only happens as funding gets tight. If it is to be truly informative it should be a regular part of committee and council work

GOD'S STORY

Home

One of the most often asked questions I get as a pastor and now as a teacher of scripture is, "How is it best to read the Bible?" Behind the question is the evangelical tradition of reading the Bible cover-to-cover each year. Many find the thought of this exercise overwhelming.

My answer usually is that there is no right way to read the Bible. As we look at the 3-year Sunday lectionary much of the scripture is covered (particularly if you utilize a semi-continuous option for the Old Testament readings). I also suggest the use of the daily lectionary (which can be found readily on-line or now in several daily planners). These provide a nice compliment to the Sunday readings. There are also a host of resources out there for the guided reading of the Bible. I have found that from time I need to break up such reading with focusing on a particular book. I practice the discipline of reading the gospel that will be featured in the lectionary cycle for that year (Mark/John, Matthew or Luke) before Advent of that year.

No matter how we choose to organize the reading of the Bible we do well when it becomes a regular, if not daily part of our life. I find it helpful to connect it with my daily devotions/meditation. Often the Bible reading helps to inform my prayer/meditation.

Regardless of the methodology there is always a tendency within the church to make the Bible a head trip. Regardless of our starting point and our best intentions we fall prey to talking *about* the Bible, *about* God, and *about* Jesus. Frankly, it's safer that way. To allow Scripture to become a matter of the heart is to open ourselves and the world to be transformed – under no circumstances should that be taken lightly!

Yet if it does not become a matter of the heart it will remain words on a page. The miracle of the Christ event is the incarnation…the Word become flesh. It is that enfleshed Word that we are called to bear to the world. As with the Greeks who came to Phillip, those who come to us come not to find out about Jesus but to encounter Jesus in the flesh and it is the earthen vessel of our flesh that Jesus has taken on. It is not a matter of getting the Scripture into our hearts but seeing the Christ who already abides there. We are but sacraments, blessed and broken, that reveal the one who dwells among us full of grace and truth.

How do we come to know this Christ who dwells in, with and under us? In the early church it was called breaking open the Word. It was the activity of the catechumenate as they gathered in preparation for baptism. They would gather around the texts that they had just heard in worship with questions very similar to those we used in the last chapter: What does this word have to say about: Who is God? Who am I? How do we live in community together? What does God want us to do with our lives?

The issue becomes for us, what does this word have to say about our lives of faith? Where does God's story meet My Story? We need to reach the point where we begin to do this questioning every time we hear scripture shared whether it is on Sunday morning in worship, in our homes for devotion, when we gather for Bible Study, or when we read scripture at the beginning of a meeting. This does not happen overnight, nor does it happen without some intentionality.

If one believes that the conversation with scripture is a "live" conversation, then the traditional way of engaging that content leaves much to be desired. Most of Biblical scholarship approaches the task with a methodology akin to an autopsy. That is not to say that the tools of Biblical scholarship are not highly useful but more critical is *how* we use them to assist us in a conversation with a dynamic Word?

I prefer to begin with the Biblical material using an inductive rather that deductive methodology. Rather than beginning with the question, "What does the text mean?" I suggest we begin with "What is the text saying to me?"

To that end I encourage the following process as a starting point for engaging the scriptures whether for devotional use, sermon preparation or serious study of the Bible:

- Read the text. Preferably out loud.
- Read the text a second time paying particular attention to words or phrases that attract your attention. Pay special attention to questions that may arise as you listen to the text. I keep a pad of paper beside me when I am doing this and write the notes down as I go.
- If I was using this exercise for devotional reading, I would use these notes as a beginning point for my meditation and prayer.
- For our purposes I suggest we use these notes, especially the questions, as an entry point into our conversation with the text.

In this way I would argue that we begin with the assumption that the text has something to say to us today as well as having had a word to say at the time of its first offering. Now we are prepared to bring the tools of our scholarship to bear as we begin to explore the mysteries of this centuries-long conversation.

Church

The central loci for encountering God's story as the church is in the *Rite of the Word*. The community gathers around a particular story. That story is explicitly shared in the readings for the day and in the preached word as well as implicitly found in the liturgy, the hymns and in the meal.

What does this portion of the liturgy look like in our weekly celebrations? It has become vogue in many places these days to truncate the reading of scripture in worship. Limit the number of readings (sometimes to one), edit the prescribed readings to eliminate unwanted or controversial parts or simply to shorten it, dispose of the psalmody or eliminate the reading of scripture all together. What do we say about the priority of the Word with practices such as these? What story do we tell? How we tend to God's story in public worship says a great deal about how we view the place of that story in our lives and what impact it might have on living in this world. How we share that story in worship also speaks volumes. Do we read it from a book, or a bulletin insert? Do we hear it from a variety of different voices (young, old, male, female)? Is the sermon always from the pulpit or delivered in the midst of the people? Are a variety of different styles of delivery used? The worship and music committee would do well to periodically ask the question, "What are we saying about God's Story?"

As we look at how to effectively encounter God's story in the life of the congregation, I believe the best approach is multifaceted and saturated. Do it whenever and wherever to opportunity arises.

- Don't wait for the pastor to tell you what the readings for Sunday morning mean. Start a group that reads the texts prior to Sunday (if your church does not provide a listing of the next Sunday's readings ask for them to be provided). Gather and sit with those readings and your questions. You will be amazed at what you begin to hear in those sermons.
- As you begin council or committee meetings use the coming Sunday's gospel reading and the questions to prepare yourselves to do the work that is before you. It might be helpful that before you begin the process you might identify the issues before you in that meeting (i.e. As we begin our devotions tonight let us remember

that we will be dealing with matters of worship planning or budget or faith formation, etc.).

- Start small group gatherings in your homes, coffee houses, restaurants with multigenerational gatherings around Scripture and your questions.
- The second part of the conversation is to recognize that it is intended to be a tri-part conversation between ourselves, the text and the community. In **Front Porchin'** I talk in terms of My Story, God's Story and Your Story. One of the struggles that pastors and Bible study leaders have with scripture study is that we tend to do our work in isolation from the community so that when we gather the community, we and they often assume we are the "expert." This is contributed to also by the Western reading of scripture that seeks the meaning of the text rather than the text as conversation starter which was the traditional Jewish way of approaching scripture (Rabbi so and so says this about the text and rabbi such and such says something a little different... Now, how do we hear the text today?).
- The textual conversation then if it is to be truly a living conversation is not simply between me and the text but also must include the community (however we define that). As Martin Luther once is reported to have said, "Those who read the Bible alone read it to their own damnation." Maybe he understood the conversation.

A simple model of inquiry is to probe the reading of scripture is to use these four questions:

- What does the passage have to say about God (Father, Son, Holy Spirit)?
- What is does the passage say about who I am?
- What word does the passage speak about how we live in community together?
- What does God want me to do?

Neighbor

Where is God leading us in the world?

All too often when we have the outreach conversation in the church (What should we be doing in the community around us?) we sound a whole lot like every social service agency already at work in the community. What do we bring to such a conversation that is not already being said/done? I would argue that it is **God's Story**. By that I do not mean what I have been subjected to by well-meaning colleagues when they lament: If we could only get Jesus back into the family, school, workplace... etc. we could bring an end to the drug problem, teen pregnancy, unemployment, crime, broken homes.... No, what I'm advocating is listening to the community *through* God's story.

As we begin to listen to the community around us let us listen with ears attuned to God's story as well as the community's story. Are there biblical images that are raised in the conversations? Do you hear overtones of being trapped like God's people in Egypt, hostages to the systems around them? Do you hear a yearning for the Good Old Days like when David and Solomon were king (days in retrospect that really weren't all that good)? Do you hear feelings of living in a strange place like our ancestors in exile? Is the community in anticipation of change (2nd Isaiah)? Is it a community trying to rebuild in the midst of devastation (3rd Isaiah)? Is the dominant question, "Why do bad things happen to good people?" Are they searching for a savior? Do they need to experience grace? Are they feeling lost (parables)? Are they facing death? Are they feeling all dried up like a valley of dry bones? The list is endless.

I would suggest that as these images/stories arise in the conversation that you suspend the conversation and explore the story more deeply, using some of the exercises from FP in the God's Story and God's Story/My Story sections to begin to wrestle with the question, "What is God trying to say to us through this story?" How then does that relate back to your discussion of the community? Are there insights to be gained? Are there other images raised? Are there other questions now surfacing?

Before jumping into action... sit and listen. You will be amazed at how much more you sound like the church when you are able to do that.

OUR STORY

Church

As we turn to the discussion of Our Story, we must rearrange our paradigm and begin our discussion with how this plays out in the gathered congregation (church). As St. Paul reminds us, we are the body of Christ. That is who we are, that is our nature. That is most evident as we gather for the Eucharist. For the past decade I have been using a quote from St. Augustine at the elevation of the bread and cup. I turn to the congregation and say, "Be what you see. Receive who you already are." We partake of the body of Christ even as we are already members of it and yet are growing into that identity more fully week by week. We tell and have **Our Story** reshaped every time we gather at table.

What is being said in the telling of that story in our celebrations? How would it be heard by one not of our particular clan? I have found travelling around to other Lutheran churches for the past decade has made me much more conscious of how we tell our story at Grace (changing those patterns and habits is not easy but until we notice them for what they are we will continue to communicate the same message intentional or not).

- How are people welcomed? I am an opponent of appointed greeters. Hospitality is the call of the whole people of God. So how would you make a guest feel welcomed in your house? What simple acts of hospitality should each member be educated in to make the stranger welcome (the cool part of hospitality is that sometimes we entertain angels without even knowing it).
- How is worship understood? Is it for the entertainment of those gathered? Is it for the egos of those leading worship? Is it to acknowledge and praise God? I have recently reintroduced an old Augustana Lutheran practice of announcing that, *"God is in his holy Temple; the Lord is with his people; the Lord is near to those who are of a humble spirit. He hears the prayers of the faithful. Let us draw near with boldness unto his throne of grace. Let us prepare our hearts and minds for worship."* at the conclusion of the announcements

as a reminder (most especially for me) as into whose presence we are assembling.

- What things are most important in worship? Sermon? Meal? Music? Comfort? Brevity? The Rite things? An honest assessment is critical. Often times we are not sure what is sacred in worship until we transgress it.
- What do the things of worship say about who we are? How is art used? What is the condition of the sanctuary? What is the focus of worship? How is the worship environment consistent or dissonant from the story you wish to tell? How do you share the meal? Is this consistent with who you are. Do you use a dime-sized wafer or a hunk of bread and what do each of these say?
- Do you use the lectionary and the liturgical seasonal calendar to assist in telling the story?
- Do you celebrate rites of passages beyond baptism, first communion and confirmation?
- How do decisions about worship happen? Pastor? Committee? Musician? What does this say about who you are?

Regularly sitting down and asking the question of what we are saying to each other, God and the world about who we are as we gather will prove instructive. I find it helpful to attend a Roman Catholic Mass periodically to experience the incongruity in their story. I am often warmly welcomed, as a Lutheran the shape of the liturgy is familiar, and the worship clues from cantors and others are usually sufficient to feel at home in worship. Just when I am beginning to feel at home the announcement is made that only Roman Catholics in good standing are welcome at the table. POW! Not my story anymore! While I have not attended a Lutheran church that has excluded me in such an in-your-face way, they have communicated that their social hour (worship) is *their* social hour and not mine in 100 different little ways.

The liturgy is **Our Story.** Not mine. Not yours. Not even God's. Our story. How we tend that story will speak volumes to both insiders and outsiders.

As we tell **Our Story** in worship what do we expect to happen? I would argue that the church has had a long-standing outcome of our gathering around the table. This is clearly stated in the final line, "Go in peace. Serve the Lord". As Christ is bread for us in the meal so we are sent out into the world to be bread (the body of Christ) for the sake of the world. We do that both as individuals and as congregations alike.

Home

Love of Neighbor

All tables for the Christian are *de facto* extensions of the Eucharist. What we do individually/family we do as the whole body of Christ. We all too often, and particularly in terms of outreach, view these separately. What we do is always part of the larger story. That larger story informs and instructs us just as our actions and words speak to that same story adding congruence or dissonance.

This point was driven home recently in a very helpful conversation with a church development person who shared his philosophy (theology) of looking at the distribution of assets at the end of our days in a wholistic fashion: family, charitable causes, institutions, etc. Should we not look at our outreach in a similar wholistic manner?

What causes do you support either monetarily or as a volunteer? How does your being part of God's Story: Inform those choices? Support you in that work? Challenge you to see the world differently? Is that story pushing you in new directions?

I have insisted that every one of these places in the world that we are involved in is a potential Front Porch which serves as a platform for us to be part of God's unfolding story. I am not saying that to be faithful we have to run around with bright yellow tee shirts announcing that we are God's Hands or that we need to name Jesus for it to be Christian discipleship. What I am saying is that when we are asked the question about why we do this work we should be ready and prepared to tell My Story...God's Story...Our Story.

Neighbor

What are the needs of the community?

In many ways everything we have talked about thus far has led us to this point. If we are conscientious in the above process then we are poised on our Front Porches ready to venture out into the world (the revelation at this point is that we are already there – in the world, that is!). At this point we could probably put together a pretty accurate assessment of the community into which we are being called. The problem is that it is ***our*** assessment... ***our*** version of their story. We need to be able to listen to their story. We can do that very effectively one-on-one where we live, work and play

Sometimes, however, we need a birds'-eye-view. One of the most effective ways to do this is for the congregation to invite segments of the community in for a forum/discussion on a particular topic. In the conversations and interactions with the community you may have discovered what you think are the needs of the community. The forum is a good way to double check your assessments as well as provide coordination/ cooperation and generate first steps.

A number of years ago we were struggling with getting a good picture of the youth not involved in our congregation that resided in our community. We invited everyone we could think of whose job entailed interacting with youth on a regular basis: Children and Youth Services, Drug and Alcohol, School teachers, the judge, law enforcement, day-care workers, mental health, counselors and parents. We asked them to address the youth population through the lenses which they most often encountered them – in short, tell us your story of youth in our community. There were two startling revelations coming out of that: First, these people rarely interacted with each other and secondly, there were several clearly defined issues facing the youth of the community which came out of those discussions. My colleague, Mark Fischer, recently held a similar forum for his community around the issue of the opioid drug issue. His experience was very similar.

As we discussed in FP, we as church are called to listen these days with three sets of ears to three sets of stories: My Story, God's Story and Your Story. Our Story grows out of the continual interplay and interweaving of these three stories. It is an ongoing process that requires practice and discipline. I designed FP as a way to begin this work within the life of the congregation. Hopefully this guide, ***Transforming Grace*** will open new doors that enable us to share the story of God as it has taken shape in our lives with others.

PART 3

BUILDING A STRONG FRONT PORCH

Sometimes our front porches become so deteriorated that they become incapable of carrying the full weight of our evangelism efforts. One of my fondest memories with my dad was the Saturday that he invited me to assist him in fixing our front porch. We ripped off the façade and exposed the decaying beams that were almost holding up the porch. We then jacked the porch off the rotting beams and replaced them with fresh lumber. In many ways this strategy is as much about shoring up our front porches to make them usable to do the work of evangelism as it is about "evangelism programming". In some cases, it is not that our front porches have deteriorated – they simply don't exist. One of the architectural phenomena of our time is the movement from front porches to secluded decks. In many ways our worshipping communities have followed suit. For some of us, therefore, this process of evangelism will also necessitate new construction or at least a revisiting of critical areas of ministry.

This section is designed to assist in a critical look at the crucial areas of ministry through a missional lens. How does the whole of congregational life support and lead us to further the work of God's kingdom where we live and work and have our being? It can be used as a total renewal process or to address specific areas of ministry than may need some shoring up. If we are to engage in God's work on the front porch then the work within the house must be strong and supportive.

Tools. It is true that a carpenter is only as good as his/her tools and also that the best tool in the hands of inexperience is not all that helpful. What tools do we as the church bring to the task of table building? The church has centered her life around seven faith practices: prayer, Bible study, worship, evangelism, mutual consolation of the brothers and sisters, service and the stewardship of God's resources. The Evangelical Lutheran Church in America refers to these practices in verb form: <u>Pray</u>, <u>Study</u>, <u>Worship</u>, <u>Invite</u>, <u>Encourage</u>, <u>Serve</u> and <u>Give</u>. The active form of these words lends a helpful sense of dynamic to our faith practices/tools. These will be the basis for our examining and building of our mission tables and our Front Porches.

Materials. Our chief material for the construction of our mission table is the body of Christ in all its expressions. First, it is the body of Christ that we refer to as Lord (*kyrios*) who we believe, teach and confess sits at the right hand of God. It is his authority and presence through the work of the Holy Spirit that enables us to undertake this project with any hopes of success. Secondly, it is the body of Christ that we know intimately as those we gather at table with each week – the brothers and sisters of our local congregation. This is a body with a particular context, story and tradition. It will be those in-grained patterns that will give our porch its distinctive grain and beauty. Finally, we are gathered together with brothers and sisters in the expression of the body of Christ that we know as judicatories. This body too has a distinctive pattern that will impact our Front Porches. It brings a larger sense of vision and also a greater wealth of resources. This is the body which gathers most fully in its catholic expression. Since we are surrounded by so great a cloud of witnesses, we do not loose heart. It is the communion of saints, not only of the church present but also of the church triumphant which surround and support us in these efforts to fulfill our calling as the body of Christ. As such gathered at our tables are the likes of Peter and Paul, Augustine and Francis, the Luthers (Martin and Katie), Bonheoffer as well as all of those saints who have led and inspired us over the years in our present settings.

Plan. Early in my tenure as a parish pastor I launched into a discussion with council one night about a long-range planning process. One of the council members (a university faculty member) cut me off and said, "We are always launching into long-range planning processes and over the years I have noted that by the time we get to implementing the plan it is already outdated!" I have found that to be a helpful insight especially in recent years where our world seems to be changing at warp speed. I am proposing a planning process that is simple, ongoing, flexible and focuses on short-term goals/results. I have engaged in enough building projects to know how often things change in the middle of the plan.

In the last few decades there has been much conversation in leadership circles around the concept of **Adaptive Leadership** (Heifetz, Grashow and Linsky). Works by John Kotter (**Leading Change** and **XLR8**) and **Canoeing the Mountains** (Tod Bolsinger) can be very helpful in negotiating the rapid changing society. It is tempting to focus on technical questions rather than addressing the adaptive questions facing the congregation. A final work that I have found helpful in this initial process is Warren Berger's, **A More Beautiful Question**. That said, let's get started...

Former Bishop and church executive, Pastor Stephen Bouman first introduced me to the concept of "Mission Table". While it runs the risk of mixing metaphors, I believe that it is the appropriate image to begin our conversation concerning the congregational household and our Front Porches.

One can legitimately argue that the table is the primary launching point for Jesus' mission in the world. It is at table that Jesus encounters sinners, outcasts, and foreigners. It is from the table that Jesus sends his disciples out to serve. It is at table that Jesus is most recognizable in his post-resurrection form.

As I read ancient liturgies and history, the gathering place of the early church (pre – 4ᵗʰ Century) was around the table. The worship of the community gathered resembled a meal far more than a show. It was around the table that community was formed, story remembered/shared, prayer was offered, and mission was conceived. I believe that the table is the starting point today as we turn our energies toward building a strong foundation for our Front Porchin'.

On the night in which he was betrayed, Jesus transformed all tables into sacred tables and all meals into holy eating. For the Christian whenever we gather to eat, we do so as an extension of the Eucharist. Where two or three gather there is Christ in the midst of them. It was at table that the disciples first recognized the Christ following the resurrection as he broke bread with them. It is at table that we most clearly re-present the risen Christ to the world today.

If this is true, how then do we build or restore our mission table for as the gathering of the whole people of God today? As an amateur furniture builder, I have made plenty of mistakes over the years but through most of them I have learned a thing or two about building. Perhaps most important is careful and thoughtful preparation (while not a failsafe good preparation has saved me many expensive miscues. The old adage measure twice cut once is critical to minimizing fruitless directions and decisions).

For centuries it has been around the table that we have formed and been formed as human communities. From intimate multi-generational family gatherings to the public banquets, society has found the table a place where formation has taken place, intentionally or unintentionally. As Christian communities of faith it has been around the communion Table where we have been called, gathered, enlightened, sanctified and kept at the church, the body of Christ. Therefore, I believe around the table is the appropriate place for us to begin our re-formation as the missional church.

We believe, teach and confess that for us as Christians all tables are a reflection and extension of that communion Table. Whenever we eat and drink together, we do so as the people gathered and sent from that common Table. As such I would like to suggest that there are two table images that might be helpful for us to understand the two-fold dynamic of mission in the name of Jesus. They are the kitchen table and the picnic table.

Kitchen Tables

There has always been a sure sign for me in my ministry that I have been accepted, "Pastor, you can use the back door." The significance of that is not the door but rather where the door led – the kitchen. Over the years my most significant conversations with people happened not in the living room or my office but rather around their kitchen table. The kitchen table has been the place in our families for generations where the work of being family is done. It is there we dare to talk about what is really on our minds and in our hearts. For that reason I believe that we need to sit down at our congregation's kitchen table together that we may talk about the most significant things we have to talk about as the people of God: who are we and what is God calling us to do in this place. The kitchen table is about faith formation.

While such tables abound in scripture one of my favorite kitchen table talks is found in the 13-17th chapters of John's gospel. This "Farewell Discourse" by Jesus is a final stage preparation/formation of the disciples/ church to carry on the mission of Jesus following his crucifixion and resurrection. All of the things that are necessary for the church's formation: Prayer (chapter 17); Worship/Community (chapter 15); Catechesis (13:31-35); Stewardship/Discipleship of Our Lives (13:1-20); Leadership Training (14:15-31; 16:1-33). Tables were the loci of the Kingdom for Jesus.

In the same way it is around the kitchen table of our congregations that we are called to engage in the hard, hot, stressful and at times costly work of ongoing preparation: prayer, worship, catechesis, stewardship and leadership development. The kitchen table calls for passion and skill. Those who are called to oversee the work of this congregation's kitchen table will need to be people who are passionate and skilled in the areas of prayer, worship, catechesis, stewardship and leadership development. Above all else they must be good cooks, that is, they must be creative and see how they complement one another in their respective callings in such a way as the meal is enhanced in its fullness.

> *One of the most successful structural changes I made in my parish ministry was the development of a committee structure not based on IBM but on the seasons of the church year. Rather than separate committees we gathered as a whole seasonally to talk about how the particular season of the church year might impact/shape how we prayed, worshiped, formed each other in faith (catechesis), lived out our call to be disciples (stewardship), and developed leaders. I am proposing that we gather around the kitchen table seasonally (Advent/ Christmas/Epiphany; Lent; Easter; Pentecost; Ordinary Time (Summer/Fall)). The makeup of those gatherings at the different seasons might be different from season to season depending upon gifts and desire (there are advent people and Easter people). (See Appendix B)*

This process is intended to walk you through a look at your kitchen table board by board. As you begin to wrestle with the questions at the end of each section the shape of your table will become clearer. It will be from this table that you will then be invited to look more carefully at your table as a mission table

To be able to witness to the presence of the crucified and risen Jesus we need to know who that Jesus is. This is the work of the Kitchen Table. But ultimately it will be around the Picnic Table that we begin to gather for mission so a brief description of this table and the interplay with the Kitchen Table is warranted before we go much any further.

Picnic Table

It was not unusual on a Sunday afternoon when I was growing up to find my mother packing the picnic basket and my father ushering my brother and me into the Buick station wagon. Off we went on an adventure (usually without much direction) driving until we found a suitable picnic table. In those days there seemed to be an inexhaustible supply of such places throughout western New York and northwestern Pennsylvania. Rarely was there just a single table either. This normally produced the second adventure...that of meeting strangers.

My mom and dad seemed to have no trouble engaging strangers in conversation to the point that before long it appeared that we had known each other for a long time. These exchanges often entailed the exchange of food. And when the food had been consumed and the tables cleared, they became places to perch and continue shared conversation.

I believe that the picnic table offers us a fitting image to gather our thoughts and efforts around when we begin as congregations to talk about mission to the world. While there is much preparation that needs to be done before heading out on a picnic (kitchen table work) we also have to leave our homes if we are to discover the picnic tables that dot our world. So too when we talk of doing mission, we have a great deal of preparation (faith formation) before we ever leave home. At the same time, we have to go out to the picnic tables of our neighborhoods if we are to experience the picnic that Christ is even now preparing. Picnic tables are about the formation of apostles (the "sent ones").

The picnic table in John's gospel is to be found in chapter six with the Feeding of the 5000. With no kitchen table at hand Jesus calls Philip and the disciples to step up and feed the multitude right there where they stand. They in turn seek out the one who was prepared (the young boy and his meager fish and bread) and it is enough. The rest of chapter six is an explication of this miracle in the larger context of Moses and the exodus. The picnic table is always "out there" in the world's wilderness where life can be messy, difficult, barren, challenging and always harboring ants and bees and rain. Yet this is where God calls us, and the Holy Spirit drives us that the flesh and blood reality of the risen Jesus may be seen by the world. It is the fulfillment of our baptismal calling: to go forth and let our lights so shine that others may see our good works and come to glorify our Father in heaven.

In the midst of chapter six there is the story of Jesus walking on the water. It is easy for us engaged in this mission work in the wilderness of NWPA to be overcome by the rolling waves and the whirling winds. Like those in the boat we need to keep Jesus' words ever before us, "It is I (*I am with you*); do not be afraid"...and like them we too shall reach the place toward which we are being called.

… to the work at hand !

Step 1 Pray

Several years ago, I built a 20'x10' "cave" in my basement. There you will find my easel, paints, knives and chisels, wood, music, books, pipe and the computer I use to do my creative writing. It is the place where I go when life gets too much to bear and I need to escape. In short, I have built the modern version of my 3-season front porch. This summer there had been a serious lack of "cave" time. I was not fully aware of how it had affected me until I was on a conference call with author, Martha Grace Reese **(Unbinding the Gospel)**. When she asked how I was doing I replied, "Empty." The word was out before I could substitute my normal reply of "Okay." We talked about it and shared prayer. By that point my other colleagues had joined the conversation.

Despite the fact that they were all coming off great vacation experiences when we began to talk about our respective work, words like dry, desolate, depressing, discouraged, lifeless, barren and stuck crept into the conversation. Martha Grace let us go with our complaining and we soon began to sound more and more like Elijah on Horeb desiring to find a nice cave to hole up in for the duration. When we had worn down, she took off the gloves, picked up a baseball bat, and drove us out of the caves we were making. Like God on Horeb she laid out an agenda and a challenge.

She called us to commit to reading the Pentecostal cult classic, **Cross and the Switchblade** (David Wilkerson). It didn't take long to discover why she called us to read the book. I realized that despite a lifetime in the church, a theological degree, an ordination to Word and Sacrament, over 30 years in the ministry and now decades of working as a spiritual director, when it came to the reality of prayer in daily life, I really wasn't terribly confident that God would answer prayer. As such I cast my prayers with the enthusiasm of the sower who went out to sow. At best I expected a one in four chance of being answered (and then probably not in the way I desired). As I read the book I took more than one hit from the cosmic 2x4 between the eyes. What did I expect from God? My answer was, "Not much."

The second part of the challenge from Martha Grace was to pray. Imagine that! The prayer was specific. It was to have three parts:

1. God, reveal to me what you want me to do this day.
2. God, enable this church to see what you are calling them to become.
3. God, send help!

We find ourselves today as congregations often running on empty. It is easy to get discouraged and throw up our hands in despair or climb into our cynical caves.

A number of years ago I was engaged in a study process for implementing the Adult Catechumenate. The leader asked us, "How many of you pray for the unbaptized to come into your fellowships or be revealed to you in your daily life?" There was a long of serious head hanging. He said "That is where you begin but before you do figure out what to do with them when they come because they will come." One of my colleagues and I knew better. We went right home and started to pray. Within a month we each had a dozen inquirers of a process we had not yet gotten planned. Lesson learned – God *does* answer prayer!

As you begin this process, I encourage you to enter into a time of prayer as a planning group, council and congregation. I offer this simple prayer to be shared and prayed in personal devotions and whenever the congregation gathers (meetings, dinners, Bible Study, worship).

Good and gracious God, we ask for your guidance as we seek to do your will: Reveal to me/us this day what you need me to be about; enable our congregation to see more clearly what you are calling us to become; and in your abundant mercy send us help to accomplish all that you call us to be and do. We pray this through Christ, our Lord. Amen

Step 2 Dream

One of my fictional heroes is Cervantes', Don Quixote de La Mancha. In the musical version of this tale Don Quixote offers a soliloquy on madness from his death bed that ends with the line, "Maddest of all is to see life as it is and not as it should be."

As inheritors of the Kingdom we are called into God's vision for this world. Our next step is to prayerfully envision what God is calling this congregation to be here in this place. What are the needs of the congregation and community? What are the resources needed to begin to address these needs? Who will be needed to do this work?

It is a time to engage in a long, loving look at the setting in which God has called you. There are many ways to study your community needs but the most successful call for us to hit the streets and talk with our neighbors. Who are they? What are they hearing? What are they experiencing? A process called One on One's is a very helpful tool to have in your tool box. (See Appendix C). In many cases we have become rootless communities of faith as our neighborhoods change around us. We must call our neighbors into the dreaming process. How do we sing the songs of faith together in this foreign land we find ourselves in.

For most of my life I have been accused of being an insane optimist. I prefer to refer to myself as an Impossible Dreamer. What dreams has God been dreaming about your community? What dreams are you willing to engage in with God? Remember! God makes all things possible.

Step 3 Start Cutting (Get to Work!)

At some point if you are going to get your porch built you must stop thinking about it and start work. The first step is to assess how much work you need or are willing to do. Will your project be new construction or renovations of outdated structures?

If you are talking about new construction or major renovations, then I would suggest that you move through this material in order. If you are looking at shoring up particular areas of ministry for mission, then I would suggest focusing just on those pieces to begin with.

At the end of each section are review/discussion questions that will help move you into planning. A simple model for planning is this list of questions:

- Where are we now?
- Where do we want to be?
- What will it take to get there?
- Who needs to be at the table to move forward?
- What gifts do we have? What gifts/skills do we need to learn or engage from the outside?
- What is the next step?

Gathered Around the Table (Worship)

From the days of my childhood when I subjected my poor parents and brother to "Living Room Eucharists" served with Ritz crackers and grape juice to chairing our Synodical Committee on Worship and Music, worship has been central to living out my understanding of what it means to be a baptized Christian today. I have always been an intense critic of the worship life of the church. At times I have been branded as dinosaur while more recently questions have been raised about whether I may have crossed over to the Dark Side of contemporary styles. The critique continues.

As I sit here at the church's primary table (The Christian community is first and foremost the community gathered around the table. In the Lutheran tradition it is a table set with Water, Word, Bread and Cup). I realize that a great deal of our missional energies are drained and many of our strategies evaporate into the black hole that I refer to as "The Worship Wars." I believe that unless we can get past this distraction and deal with the heart of our worship all conversations around the kitchen and picnic tables will in the end be fruitless.

<u>**ASKING THE RIGHT QUESTIONS**</u>

In conversations with councils and evangelism committees in large congregations and the smallest of rural congregations I have found that whenever the issue of evangelism/mission surfaces sooner or later the conversation turns in one of two directions (sometimes both): 1) The "Mega Church down the road and its exciting/damned praise style of worship or 2) "We need to explore adding a contemporary worship service." Occasionally a group will focus on orthodox worship practices but in "evangelism settings" that's rare.

These conversations assume that evangelism/mission and contemporary worship are synonymous. A corollary assumption is that liturgical worship is anti-missional or at the very least becomes an impediment. The truth is that there is no one worship style that enables mission.

The second issue with much of the worship/mission conversation is that it really is focused on the institutional church and not on mission. True mission/outreach is not about, "How do we get people to come to our church?" (This is often the underlying premise of the contemporary worship question) but rather "How do we share the good news of Jesus Christ with those who have never heard? (This may indeed be happening in the context of your worship, but it is not guaranteed).

When we start off with such assumptions and questions it is no wonder our conversations quickly become arguments that either divide or derail congregational efforts to do mission (sometimes they are the perfect scapegoat for a congregation that plays the missional lip service game – we tried!). I believe that if we are serious about wrestling with our worship lives and our lives in mission (which is after all one life) then we would do well to focus our discussion around two words: Presence and Passion.

PRESENCE

Whether our preference is the "highest" of liturgical styles replete with the accompanying smells and bells or the "contemporary informality" of Praise Worship accompanied with guitars, drums and backup vocals, as I listen to the conversations I realize that much of our worship has a misplaced object. Our worship conversations have a great deal to do with us and very little these days with God. Instead of worshipping God we succumb to the idolatry of worshipping our worship or some other idol.

I believe the key to fighting this temptation and to being faithful to our call as evangelists (good news speakers) is found in the mystery of the incarnation (*God in flesh*). While we trot the doctrine of the incarnation out each Christmas, we rarely take it seriously. Interestingly, the only times I have ever stirred opposition to a sermon was when I pushed the "incarnation button" (once I suggested that Mary must have had a struggle with Jesus as he went through the terrible twos and the other when I suggested that Jesus had doubts and fears on the cross). We have become functional deists. We desire a God removed from our spheres of influence (except when we need God – a kind of "Don't call me, I'll call you" relationship). The incarnation plops the Divine right down in the muck and mire of our daily existence...that's a little too close for most of us! (That is especially true when it comes to our worship life).

A brief missional moment. If we take seriously the incarnation of John 1 (...the Word became flesh and dwelt among us) and its attendant parallel in Genesis 1 (...let us create humanity in image) then our task of evangelism is not to bring some foreign/outside word to bear on people's lives but to speak to the presence of God in Christ that is already there... it is in a sense about uncovering... of revealing the truth that has been hidden to this person. Conversion then is to begin to see ourselves as God sees us and has from the beginning. Evangelism then in short is an encounter of the Christ in me and the Christ that dwells already in the other. The most effective arena for this evangelism is not in worship but in our service. I believe that the model Jesus lays before us of this is best illustrated in John when Jesus hikes up his robe, rolls up his sleeves, wraps a towel around his waist and begins to wash his disciples' feet. That he feels compelled to command his disciples/us to do this (have love for one another as I have for you) testifies to the centrality of the church's witness in service. It is in the encounter with our brothers and sisters outside of the church that we most intimately encounter the risen Christ (scars and all). So what of worship?

If we encounter Christ/God in the face of those we live, work and play with then why go to church? Why worship? We worship for all those reasons we have traditionally lifted up: praise, thanksgiving, catechesis etc. I would argue, however, that the primary reason we need to come together to worship is that we come to see Jesus in a way that we cannot do for each other. In the context of worship, we are encountered by the Divine presence, exposed if you would, removed from the messiness of our human bodies. God reveals himself in a piece of bread and a sip of wine, a splash of water a word spoken and yet is not confined to those physical elements. While Christ makes himself present in, with and under these forms the divine presence is not limited by those forms. Christ also is present in the one who presides, present in the one who prays, present in the one who sings, present in the one who makes music, present in the one who offers hospitality, present even in the one who disrupts and yet Christ is not limited to these forms either. The Christ who greets us in worship comes as the one we anticipate – this one comes in glory and power and dominion...this is the one of whom Handel writes when he pens his Halleluiah Chorus..."and He shall reign..." This is the awesome presence of Yahweh's Shekaina (glory) as it booms from Sinai and the "crushing silence" that grips Elijah at the mouth of the cave. This is an uncomfortable presence for it calls for our continual conversion...our continual growing into who we are called to be as the people of God. Is it any wonder we try to cover up this God with our liturgies and bands?

PASSION

This passionate God comes to us in worship and calls us into a passionate encounter. Yet in most of our worshipping bodies our response leaves something to be desired: In liturgical churches we worry about how the liturgy gets done. In Praise churches we worry about how good is the band. In between all too often it's a matter of getting through this worship stuff in an hour.

What is it to be passionate about worship? When I first began to explore this question my high church sensibilities were sorely rocked. Try as I might I could find little passion in my beloved liturgical tradition. What I did find was anxiety about getting it right and angst when things were not as they were supposed to be. I had to admit to myself that perhaps the contemporary worship folks did have the answer. Maybe theirs was a worship of passion. Then more recently I read the summary report of a congregation with a long-standing history of Praise worship. Repeatedly, comments were made of the succession of pastors that they either possessed or did not possess the energy necessary for Praise worship. Energy is not passion.

To speak of passion in worship we need only to seek the one who comes to us passionately, for answers.

It is in the Passion, the incredible and vulnerable exposure of God in Christ's crucifixion and death that provides the clues. To be passionate before this God is to allow ourselves to be vulnerable. How do we come to the Garden sans our fig leaves? The question is not, "How comfortable does our worship make us?" or "How meaningful it is?" or "How much we were entertained by the 'Jesus Show." No, the question becomes, "How does what we do in worship leave us exposed and vulnerable before the passionate God who has come to encounter us?"

It is here where presence and passion kiss. Our worship is a present event. The God that greets us there greets us in the present – not the past – not the future. The great mystery of our faith, "Christ has died, Christ is risen, Christ will come again," becomes true and real in each celebration of our Eucharistic gathering. Past and future become present.

Our liturgical and pietistic traditions are important not because they are part of the church's past (they are not holy relics). Rather they are valuable for us because over the course of church history they have shown the ability to reveal to us the passionate God who makes himself known to us in the breaking of bread. In like manner contemporary worship is not necessarily present worship if it provides no opportunity for God to get a word in edgewise.

Whatever the "style" of worship, what we must focus on is how well the worship allows for us to dwell in the encounter with the passionate presence of Christ. This is a much more difficult task. It requires those who plan and lead worship to have a dwelling relationship with that same passionate presence in their daily lives. It means when gathering for worship planning it is done in the context of dwelling with this passionate presence. It means listening and dwelling in that word made flesh to shape the "style" of a particular worship experience. It means that at some times of the year or certain celebrations smells and bells may be the order of the day. On other celebrations an attitude of unabashed praise may be what is called for. They key is always pointing to the passionate presence and then getting out of the way.

In the history of the church, when the worshipping community was able to do this effectively, they were also effective evangelists and mission oriented. One leads to the other. Our learning to encounter the Divine in our brothers and sisters in the midst of our witness drives us to be more open in our encounters with that passionate presence that grips us as we gather in the community of the baptized. In like manner, that gathering together in the passionate presence of Christ compels us into the world in such a way that our response to the dismissal, "Go in peace. Serve the Lord" is met with an enthusiastic, "Thanks be to God."

Questions for Review

a. *What are the strengths of our present worship?*
b. *What are we not pleased with, or what is no longer working?*
c. *How does/doesn't our worship tie in with God's mission to the world?*
   3 things that would make worship more integral to mission in our congregation.
d. *Are there other worship experiences that you would like to try in the next year?*
e. *What assistance from the synod do you desire as you reflect on your worship life?*

Voices Around The Table (Study)

When we gather around the table, we are shaped by the voices that also gather around that table with us. It was around the kitchen table that I learned who I was. It was there I heard the stories of the family, both past and present. It was there that I discovered the behaviors that were expected of me. It was in that community of voices that I was shaped.

When we have talked about faith formation in the past, we have narrowly confined it to that hour block of time on Sunday morning affectionately known as Sunday School. As such the construct of our conversation has been "educational" (the transfer of information about God, Jesus and the faith). We have done a particularly good job of this style of faith education. But faith formation is a larger task than the transmittal of information. For that reason, I prefer to use the word "catechesis" for the work of the church in forming faith. Catechesis literally means "sounding in one's ear". How appropriate for voices gathered around the table. It assumes that all the voices around the table are important and that all of those gathered around the table will be formed/transformed in their faith journey together by this conversation.

One of the most powerful loci for this conversation is around the worship table. We have often underestimated the power of our liturgy, music and prayers in the catechetical process. How often we have segregated catechesis from worship (at least in our minds). The worship table is one of the most critical voices around our catechetical table. That is particularly, but not exceptionally, true of the so-called liturgical churches. We might be shocked to recognize how much of our personal theology (understanding of God, Christ and church) has been shaped by the liturgy and hymnody. Our "favorite" hymns probably say a lot about how we have constructed the faith. That is why an exclusive diet of Praise Songs becomes as issue because it provides little content for the grist mill of catechesis. The first place we should look in examining our catechetical process is our worship. What are we saying about God, Jesus, the church, our gathered community (who gets included and how?), and the world in our dress, words and actions (both formal and informal or scripted and unscripted)? This should be the first agenda item on any catechetical conversation.

Sociologists point to one of the markers of community as having a common story (meta-narrative). The common story or the Voice of voices is the story of the Judeo/Christian tradition in its fullest form, the Word of God. I do not narrowly define this as simply confines to the pages of scripture but also speak of the work of the Holy Spirit in the gathered community of Word and Sacrament. How is this story told? What are the nuances to that story in our context? Is it a story (as popular indictments accuse us) of "Thou shall not's..." and exclusivity? Is it a story of the love of God for his people through Jesus? Is it a moral code? Is it information about God, Jesus, Holy Spirit, personalities of the Bible, and history? Is it a story that invites discussion or cuts it off? Is it a word that transforms? How do we speak of the Hebrew Scriptures (the Old Testament) in relation to the New Testament? In addition to this meta-narrative we have our denominational story (For me, what is the place of the Lutheran Confessions around the table?), and our local story (Who are we here at St. John's by the Gas Station?). What is the place of these stories and their traditions in the conversation around the Table?

Recently I was invited into a congregation to, "...tell us about any of the new and innovative offerings in adult education... and, O by the way, we'd like more information on that adult catawhatchamacallit ... you know, the thing you talk about." I had 15 minutes on the agenda.

What they were looking for was a miracle... something to rejuvenate a dying program in four easy steps. As I sat down to discern where I was to go with the presentation I was struck with an interesting synthesis.

For the past 15 years I have been working with the adult catechumenate model for baptismal preparation and faith formation including a short stint with the Evangelical Lutheran Church in America's introduction team for Welcome to Christ. While the integrity of the process as a baptismal process is critical I believe that the process has more to say to us today. I believe that in the midst of our struggles with Sunday School, intergenerational and adult education this process is a voice we need to listen to. I believe that it can provide for us the shape for a more effective approach to catechesis in our congregations.

In my reflection I became aware that each of the four movements within the process (inquiry, catechumenate, purification and mystagogy) should be present at all times within the overall catechetical ministry of our congregations. One of our problems is trying to create a program/ class/offering to meet everyone's needs and in the end, it may meet no more than our own personal needs. At any time in our faith journey we can find ourselves needing to revisit (or visit for the first time) any one of these movements. If we can offer opportunities in each of these areas we open up the potential to reach more people where they find themselves on their journey.

I would like to walk through each of these four movements and then offer some possibilities of practices that you might introduce or adapt for your situation. There are four legs to the journey each marked by an appropriate rite. These are:

Inquiry
Catechumenate
Purification and Enlightenment
Mystagogy

The ***Period of Inquiry*** is the initial stage of the journey. It has no prescribed time limits. It is a time when those who are experiencing an awakening faith come with their questions and inquiry about the Christian faith. It is a time to build trust and to share personal stories. During this part of the journey they begin to hear the message of salvation and experience the first pangs of conversion. It is a time to introduce them into congregational life.

Through discernment the inquirer may come to recognize his or her desire to continue this journey in a more formal sense. At this time the congregation makes plans to welcome them into the process in a formal and public way through the Rite of Welcome. At this point the inquirer, now called a catechumen, enters into the ***Period of the Catechumenate***. This period may last from one to several years depending on the candidate. It is a time to deepen the initial conversion and to pass on the Christian faith and tradition. The candidates will engage in the life of the community in prayer, worship and service. The catechesis (teaching) is based on the Liturgy of the Word. The candidate will receive a sponsor at this time who will accompany them throughout the remainder of their journey.

Following the discernment of the catechist, sponsor, pastor, and the candidate, (and in our case also the church council), the candidate is invited to celebrate the Rite of Enrollment where they publicly declare their intentions to journey toward the baptismal waters. This rite is a powerful witness of the community on behalf of the candidate and a decisive step on the part of the candidate. This rite usually takes place on the First Sunday of Lent. Lent then becomes the context for the ***Period of Purification and Enlightenment***. The elect (no longer candidates) join the congregation in a forty-day retreat where the effort is to eliminate what is weak and sinful and to affirm what is holy. It is a time for recollection and the final preparation for the celebration of the initiation into the Sacraments.

The Sacrament of Baptism and the reception of First Communion is traditionally celebrated at the Easter Vigil. The great 50 days of the Easter season constitute the ***Period of Mystagogy***. During this period of the journey the newly baptized (neophytes) are invited to reflect more deeply on the Sacraments. The newly baptized also begin to discern their ministry in the community/congregation. The choosing of their vocations is celebrated on Pentecost Sunday as we gather to celebrate the outpouring of the Holy Spirit. The texts for this journey are: The Bible, the hymnal (color optional), Luther's Small Catechism, and the life of the community of faith.

I believe that if we are open to the Spirit's promptings then we probably would cycle through this process (informally) several times along our baptismal journey. As such I believe that it is critical for a good catechetical program to have offerings reflected in all four of the stages (at any point in our lives we might be in one or another of these) as well as a structured process for baptismal/confirmation preparation.

Below are the elements of each of the stages as they might be reflected in a catechetical curriculum:

Inquiry Catechesis Sessions

The period of inquiry should be relaxed and informal. This is a time of testing the waters. As the group develops the sessions may be driven by the group's interests or questions. Things that might be helpful:

- Sharing of stories. How did you get to this place in your journey of faith?
- Journaling
- Church tour
- Congregational History

- Meet the congregation. Invite different people from the congregation to come in and share their faith stories.
- Review the Liturgical Year
- Sharing of photos
- Current Events
- Church Trivia
- Introduction to Scripture
- Prayer

Catechumenate Catechesis Sessions

This period centers on "breaking open the Word" or reflective scripture study.

- Opening Prayer
- Reading of the text
- Initial sense of the text by the group
- Life Issues Raised by the Text (catechist will need to do their homework)
- Dialog with the text (What does the text say about these issues?)
- Integration (Does the Word challenge present realities for the catechumens?)
- How does this all get lived out in the tradition of the church?
- Mission: What does the text call us to do with our lives?
- Closing Prayer

Purification/Enlightenment Catechesis Sessions

This time should be as much like a 40 Day retreat as possible. Involve the congregation and/or design a complementary Lenten process for them. You may choose to use the Gospel readings for Cycle A as an outline and focus on Temptation, Spirit, water, Light and New Life. Focus on prayer. Explore the variety of prayers and praying (e.g. Contemplative prayer, prayer books, etc.). Keep in minds that the focus especially in this time is not the head but the heart.

Mystagogy Catechesis Sessions

The focus on this time is unpacking of the Baptismal and Eucharistic Rites that they have experienced at the Vigil. One parish I know used a weekend post-Easter retreat to provide the setting for this. Be creative. Time also should be spent on assisting the newly baptized in their selection of vocations.

An Inquiry-type event/offering might look like an informal group gathered to talk about the faith/church. It might be intergenerational (it always helps to keep the kids involved lest the adults begin to take themselves too seriously). Catechumenate-type session might easily replace the time-worn Bible study or Sunday School class curriculum. A Purification/Enlightenment Session might be a Lenten retreat or a series on prayer/spirituality. A Mystagogy-style offering might be a series of events focused on worship and the sacraments. The possibilities are limited only by one's imagination.

Having briefly looked at the traditional shape of the catechumenate model I would like to suggest that an effective use of this model is to adapt it as an ongoing faith formation process within the life of the congregation. I would argue that a healthy formation process within a congregation would have elements of each of these four movements operating at all times. Below I offer some suggestions as to what this might look like in each of the movements.

Inquiry

In many of our congregations what passes for the period of inquiry is called either "Pastor's Class" or "New Members' Class." While these can be effective tools, I am finding that fewer and fewer people are wandering into the church for worship and hence inquiry within the confines of the church building is becoming less and less viable.

I believe we begin by gathering a handful or so of our friends, workers, family (anyone we truly care about) around a table. (I am speaking not first and foremost of the marble altars that adorn our churches but rather the ordinary tables that call us together. It may be a booth at McDonalds, or a counter at the coffee shop. They are the kitchen tables in our homes and apartments. A cafeteria table at school or work also serves the purpose well. The coffee table in the living room or the TV trays that open and fold so conveniently work well to bring us together. A park bench or a picnic table also serves to gather the hungry. Within the congregation it might be the lounge or a Sunday School table. Wherever two or three gather... it is here that we begin the work of the gospel). Before we go any further it would serve us well to remember that the work around the table is first and foremost the work of the Holy Spirit. While the table very well be the arena for conversion it is not our task to make it happen. Our task is to set the table...the Spirit will serve up the Meal.

Our task is to foster a caring community around the table. True community work takes time. It requires getting to know one another, sharing hopes and dreams, fears and tears, in short it is trust building. In a society of rampant individualism (and yet a profound hunger for relationship) I believe the church not only has a mandate but is empowered to convene these fledgling communities around the table. While these tables are living communities, it should not be expected that they will grow significantly in numbers. Trust, safety and security are paramount, and this will require a consistent gathering. Remember we are not starting new churches at these tables but rather being the authentic church in the world. Over time these groups may come to pray together and seek to care for each other's needs as well as responding to the needs of a larger community (church, community, world) but this cannot be programmed.

These offerings are an opportunity to explore the stirrings of the Holy Spirit that those gathered may be experiencing. It is a time of trust building, story sharing, questioning and an introduction into congregational life. Some gathered may desire to go deeper into their relationship with God that could lead them into a more intentional engagement with a larger faith community or expression of the church.

When this occurs outside of the church setting the first movement often is not to the worshipping community. Christian worship is the primary arena for conversion and those who are growing into the faith recognize this intuitively and may be overwhelmed or intimidated by the experience of worship. It may be a more pastoral invitation to encourage them to enter the life of the congregation through such things as a men's or woman's fellowship group, a spirituality group/discussion, a Bible Study, a work projector mission trip or a group that is formed around an inquiry model within the church. This allows them to ease into the community and to begin establishing a support group within the community. These larger relationships will be critical as they move through the faith formation process.

Another opportunity for those already in the worshipping fellowship might be an annual or monthly "festival celebration" around the elements of "inquiry."

- Sharing of stories. How did you get to this place in your journey of faith?
- Journaling
- Church tour
- Congregational History
- Sharing of photos
- Current Events
- Church Trivia
- Introduction to Scripture
- Prayer

Catechumentate

The movement of the catechumenate most resembles those activities associated with Christian Education. Classes on special topics, Bible studies, Sunday School, Book Clubs etc. can be the meat and potatoes of the catechumenate.

The temptation in this period is to return to a head content model. I would encourage you that as you do Bible Study that you blend both some of the exercises from the "God Story" section of Front Porchin' with other more content-driven studies. Frustrated by appropriate Scripture studies I wrote, **Holy Talk: An Introduction to Scripture for the Occasionally Biblically Embarrassed** to provide an appropriate resource for this period. It was my intention to blend some serious head study with a more heart-centered approach.

One of the most helpful resources in approaching Lutheran doctrine during this period is a resource entitled, **Praying Luther's Small Catechism**

(Roy Beutel). Similar resources are available for other denominations as well.

Whatever material you may choose to cover during this period should be light on didactic and heavy on reflection and interaction. A helpful biblical image for me during this period is God giving the prophets the Word to chew on. Our task is to ensure maximum chewing.

Purification

The period of purification and enlightenment should resemble a 40-day Lenten Retreat. It is helpful that the whole congregation be invited into this process. Again, the aim of this period is to more fully engage the heart as well as the head in a life of faith. I have used an adaptation of the Orthodox tradition of a Pre-Lenten Retreat on a Friday/Saturday schedule to prepare for the actual Lenten retreat time. A very helpful resource for the Lenten piece is Martha Grace Reese's series **Unbinding the Gospel**. The 40-day prayer experience (**Unbinding the Heart**) that she offers has been helpful for many congregations to engage in when trying to focus on the spiritual aspects of the individual and gathered community. Personally, I have found it helpful to set up the 40-day prayer experience by working through her **Unbinding the Soul: Your Experiment in Prayer and Community.**

Mystagogy

Mystagogy is literally, the breaking open of the mysteries of faith. In the catechumenal process it is the reflection on the Sacraments which the catechumen has recently received: Baptism and Eucharist/Communion.

In a broader congregational setting, a mystagogical approach might be a series on the sacraments and/or worship. Once again, a word of caution, the question that is brought to bear should be: What have I experienced? rather than, what does this mean? The latter question is much more appropriate to address during the period of the catechumenate.

A second focus might be to offer opportunities to explore your faith through the arts. I have had the privilege of having a professor of art history at my disposal who can highlight religious themes throughout the development of art. One can also offer opportunities to learn/develop one's own artistic abilities in visual media, music, drama, and dance.

The important theme in mystagogy is that you cannot explain a mystery... you can only enter into one.

I believe this synthesis of approaches to our faith formation process in the congregation will open some new and creative opportunities. By providing offerings from all four stages of faith development we offer ongoing opportunities for entry not only by members of the congregation but also those seeking to deepen their relationship with God. Our faith journey is rarely linear but rather cyclical. Each time we move through it we are drawn as individuals and congregations deeper into the mystery that is God.

Questions for Review

    a. *What are the strengths of our present catechetical process?*
    b. *What are we not pleased with, or what is no longer working?*
    c. *How does/doesn't our catechesis/study tie in with God's mission to the world?*
        i. *3 things that would make catechesis more integral to mission in your congregation.*
    d. *Are there other catechetical experiences that you would like to try in the next year?*
    e. *What assistance from the synod do you desire as you reflect on your catechetical life?*

Listening Around the Table (Spiritual Formation)

As we began this journey on our Front Porch, we did so by looking at the three stories: My Story, God's Story, Your Story.

Critical in the spiritual formation movement from head to heart is the transition between My Story and God's Story. I did not fully understand this movement until I enrolled in a four-year program to become a certified spiritual director. In that time, I learned and practiced the art of action/reflection. The core question in this process is: Where do I see God in my life today? I have found that reflection on this question in an intentional and regular way has brought God's Story and

My Story more into relationship with one another and as such God has become more the subject of My Story than myself. As that has happened it is far easier for me to share God's Story because it is no longer distinct from mine. It also happens in a more natural and less programmed way.

This reflection can take place both in an individual as well as a group setting. I have found value in having both opportunities. Individually, it can be a general reflection on the day's events around the question of where God was present in the midst of your day. It can also include a reflection on a scripture reading where the question is modified to: What is God saying to me in this passage in my life today?

A form of review that I have adapted from Ignatian Spirituality uses these questions:

This day...

- What am I most grateful for?
- What do I want for myself?
- In what ways have I experienced God's love?
- What choices have been inadequate responses to God's love?
- How will I let God lead me into a brighter tomorrow?

A group process (and this could be used around those inquiry tables once trust is built) that I have used is this:

- Preparation: Take a piece of paper and write the first names of each member of the group   (include your own).
- Someone offers a brief prayer.
- Ten minutes of silent reflection on the past 24 hours: Where was God present in my life?
- Then in turn each member of the group shares one specific experience (keep it short and to the point!). If a person is struggling with finding one, they may simply say "Pass" and move on to the next person.
- As the person is sharing the rest of the group is listening to them and to God. When the person is finished take time to write what

you heard...it may be an image, a Bible passage, a hymn/song, a line from a poem, a movie...next to their name. When all have finished writing move to the next person. (Do not share what is written at this time).

- When all have shared begin with the first person who shared and go around the group and share what was written (no commentary or judgments about what was said and no conversation between group members). The person receiving these gifts writes them down next to their name to be taken to prayer and reflection). Again, the "Pass" rule also applies here...if you heard nothing as you listened simply say, "Pass".
- When all have shared. Someone close with a brief prayer.

A concrete example from a recent session I was involved in might be helpful in fleshing out this process: I shared that I was feeling like I was in transition, but I didn't know what God had in mind for me. One response was, "Jake, I heard in what you said the image of a threshold...stay a while in the threshold" Another offered the image of the Sun Gate from her recent trip to Machu Picchu in Peru. Another offered, "Jake, I heard the word from the psalm, "For God alone my soul in silence waits."

While this spiritual formation piece can be programmed into the catechetical/study life of our congregations it needs to be more pervasive in the overall life and vision if we are to be bold in our mission. That said, I believe that as we become more comfortable with talking about our faith experiences with one another around the Kitchen Table of our congregations we will find setting the Picnic Tables in our neighborhoods less of a daunting task.

Questions for Review:

a. *What are the strengths of our present spiritual formation?*
b. *What are we not pleased with, or what is no longer working?*
c. *How does/doesn't our spiritual formation p tie in with God's mission to the world?*
    i. *3 things that would make spiritual formation more integral to mission in your congregation.*

    d. *Are there other spiritual formation experiences that you would like to try in the next year?*

    e. *What assistance from the synod do you desire as you reflect on your spiritual formation?*

The Big Table (Mission Interpretation/Give)

One of the touchiest if not downright controversial discussions around our Kitchen Table these days is that of Mission Support (regular giving beyond the congregation). The question is: How do we see ourselves in the context of the ministry of the wider church? This can take the context of local ecumenical efforts, regional, church-wide, or national/international ecumenical mission efforts. The answer to this question is critical in how we see ourselves and how we present ourselves to others around the mission of the church. I have intentionally chosen to talk about mission interpretation/support before mission because I believe how we answer that question impacts how we do mission and how we see our mission in the world. This conversation constitutes yet another layer of that story that shapes us. We are not isolated congregations but as we believe, teach and confess part of the one, holy catholic and apostolic church. Does our behavior support our confession or contradict it?

How do we talk about our relationship with the church catholic around our tables these days? In the midst of growing economic stress and church politics we have not done well with this question. One of the hardest realities of my new position both and its synodical as well as its national expression it that I have had to come to grips with the fact that the church is larger than the ecclesiastical ghetto of Grace Lutheran Church in Clarion, Pennsylvania. There are things about that insight that give me cause for celebration and at other times tears, but both testify to the truth of that reality. I can no longer pretend that the whole church is like "my" church (I may still wish that to be true, but it isn't). As mission interpreters for the whole church we must accept that for some that realization of a church other than "my" church concept is threatening to their self-understanding as a participant around the Kitchen Table. A wider-vision of the church will call our parochial view of church into question. I believe that many of us have failed to grasp the impact that has on many who gather with us.

Before we can begin the mission interpretation/support discussion we must first have the vision of the church discussion. How do we see "church"? How do we see ourselves as part of that church? What are our responsibilities to that church? What are that church's responsibilities to us? How big is my vision of the church? Once we have begun to identify how big our church is individually and collectively, we can begin to talk about the support of that church's mission.

Assuming for a moment that we are by nature parochial let us begin locally. The first step in the conversation might be to begin to invite the congregation to think of mission support as something beyond keeping the doors of the church open (which is demanding more and more of our membership each year). I would encourage beginning with one project to support in the community. We have designated one local agency (in our case a domestic violence agency) to be our community outreach which we support with personnel, monetary contributions, building space and in-kind donations. A local food bank, a community shelter, feeding program for the hungry might also be local options to expand the conversation of mission.

A second step would then to begin to look at ministry beyond the local congregation to regional mission opportunities. How are the contributions to mission support used to do mission in our synod (or respective judicatories)? How is it being used to support the camps and social agencies of the church on the territory? How is it used to promote evangelism, youth ministry, campus ministry, and congregational support? One of the examples of this has been a tie between our Sunday School and the synod's ministry to our companion synod in Tanzania. They are using a curriculum that is focusing on issues of hunger and poverty and then tying that in with supporting the Girl's School in Tanzania as well as World Hunger and Heifer International.

As often happens, synodical mission leads to a widening vision into church-wide and international mission. I have found one of the most important pieces in making this transition is to identify the mission of the wider church with a face. My apologies to all those who work so hard in church-wide offices to provide beautiful interpretation pieces (many of which attempt to identify mission with individual stories) but if you can put a local face on a church-wide mission who knows how far that might take a congregation. Following Hurricane Katrina two of our members spent three months outside New Orleans working in a Lutheran Disaster Relief (LDR) sponsored shelter and recovery facility. Last year they made a presentation to the congregation on their experiences. In a moment of divine inspiration, I grabbed a LDR offering envelope and said, "This is the kind of ministry that your dollars given to LDR go to support." When the earthquake in Haiti all I did was to point out where the envelopes could be found, and the response was overwhelming. A similar connection with World Hunger occurred following our sponsorship of a domestic World Hunger grant for the local women's shelter.

Questions for Review:

    a. *What are the strengths of our present Mission Support?*
    b. *What are we not pleased with, or what is no longer working?*
    c. *How does/doesn't our Mission Support tie in with God's mission to the world?*
        i. *3 things that would make Mission Support more integral to mission in your congregation.*
    d. *Are there other Mission Support experiences that you would like to try in the next year?*
    e. *What assistance from the synod do you desire as you reflect on your Mission Support?*
    f. *What is our percentage of Operating Expenses that will be used for Mission Support?*

Sent From the Table (Mission/Invite)

In the words of Yogi Berra, Its déjà vu all over again! We return as we began to our Front Porches. Hopefully, more prepared now to engage in the work of the kingdom in the world.

As we are gathered at the table, so we are sent from it to go in peace and to serve the Lord. Ultimately our Kitchen Table conversations propel us out into the world to do the work of the kingdom. To be faithful we cannot stay we must go and tell. Jesus sends us out into the world to announce that the kingdom of God has come near, turn around and see it coming among you. It is made visible in our mission. The great heresy of the consumer-driven church is its inward focus...what do I get out of church? The kingdom church, or the church of the Picnic Table/Front Porch, asks how might I now embody this Jesus/kingdom in the world in my daily life?

St. Francis reminds us that sometimes these efforts might even require us to use words. Whenever we engage in a Habitat project or serve a meal for the hungry, we proclaim the presence of Christ in the world. In our giving and in our acts of kindness to the neighbor we set the table.

Mission in the world is about faithfully tending the conversations around the Kitchen Table of our congregations as well as consistently and persistently looking for opportunities to set the Picnic Tables in our community.

The picnic tables of the 21st Century are the tables of the coffee shops in our communities, the counter at the local dinner, the bleachers at the stadium, the park benches, the checkout line at WalMart, the gathering of parents waiting to pick up their school children, the cafeteria at work, the classroom, the service counter, the break room, and the list goes on... The question is not, "How do we witness in these venues?" (For we witness regardless of our efforts or lack thereof). The question, and the challenge before us is, "How do we witness to the presence of the crucified and risen Jesus in these places in a way that is faithful to his life in, with and under us?"

Those called to the picnic table of our congregations will need first and foremost passion for the crucified and risen Jesus and secondly passion for their brothers and sisters who may not recognize this presence in their lives (love of Christ/love of neighbor). The other common gift is an appreciation for the work of the Holy Spirit in this process. Like Jesus we are driven by that Spirit into the wilderness of this world where our sense of self and church will be challenged but never are we alone/orphaned. The Spirit is in, with and under all that we do. Without that understanding we would become discouraged. The other gifts needed around the picnic table are discernment (picking the right spot for the picnic); an understanding of how communities work; a heart for service; enthusiasm; an understanding of how to effect change; the ability to dream dreams and the willingness to see visions. (***Front Porchin'*** was designed to assist in fostering this passion and providing an arena to talk about the intersection of faith and community).

The initial work of this table may be defining your "parish," the place to which God has called this congregation. (A helpful resource I have used to do this is "Parish as Place" by Harvey S. Peters, Jr. 1986). A next step might be intentional interviews with key leaders and neighbors around three basic questions:

From your perspective, what are the major issues facing this community?

How could the church be helpful in addressing these issues?

What do you think the overall impression of this congregation is in the community? What are we know for/as?

Interviews should include people like: the mayor, borough/city council members, commissioners, supervisors, teachers, law enforcement, business owners as well as members of the parish area. This information is vital as you move forward in creating your mission plan.

Following a conversation on Kitchen and Picnic Tables one local pastor took the concept to her congregation and they developed it quite literally. Once a month this summer they have literally sent a picnic table in the community park adjacent to the church and invited the neighborhood to join them. The pastor remarked that the following week after their first effort when she left the church those playing in the park stopped and waved to her (that had never happened before). As the summer has gone on some have shown up for worship leading to a whole new kind of conversation for this congregation around the Kitchen Table (What does the mean? What do we do now? – a great problem to wrestle with!). Who knows what will happen next... but set the tables, build the Front Porches and the Spirit will blow you off of them and into the world...on that I am convinced.

Questions for Review:

What is our "parish"?
What are the strengths of our present mission to the parish?
What are we not pleased with, or what is no longer working?

3 things that would make mission to the parish more integral to mission in your congregation.
Are there other mission to the parish experiences that you would like to try in the next year?

Step 4 Finishes

As you begin to gather direction from these Kitchen Table conversations it is helpful to begin to organize this material in a way that is useful for planning. The first step would be to collate the answers to the various questions from each section.

A second step is to assess the material and proposals coming out of each of those areas of ministry. I have found that a process called SWOT Analysis can be helpful. An intentional look at our strengths, weaknesses, opportunities and threats can be eye-opening. An example of this schematic is found in Appendix D.

A third step is the formulation of goals. How do you know what kind of goals to set? The whole point of setting goals, after all, is to *achieve* them. It does you no good to go to the trouble of calling meetings, hacking through the needs of your congregation, and burning up precious time, only to end up with goals that aren't acted on or completed.

The best goals are *smart* goals —. SMART is a handy acronym for the five characteristics of well-designed goals.

Specific: Goals must be clear and unambiguous; vagaries and platitudes have no place in goal setting. When goals are specific, they tell us exactly what is expected, when, and how much. Because the goals are specific, you can easily measure your progress toward their completion.

Measurable: What good is a goal that you can't measure? If your goals are not measurable, you never know whether you are making progress toward your successful completion. Not only that, but it's tough for you to stay motivated to complete your goals when you have no milestones to indicate their progress.

Attainable: Goals must be realistic and attainable. The best goals require you to stretch a bit to achieve them, but they aren't extreme. That is, the goals are neither out of reach nor below standard performance.

Goals that are set too high or too low become meaningless, and you naturally come to ignore them.

Relevant: Goals must be an important tool in the grand scheme of reaching your company's vision and mission.

Time-bound: Goals must have starting points, ending points, and fixed durations. Commitment to deadlines help to focus your efforts on completion of the goal on or before the due date. Goals without deadlines or schedules for completion tend to be overtaken by the day-to-day crises that invariably arise in a congregation.

Finally, we are ready to compile a *Congregational Mission Plan.* There are four questions around which to center your discussions.

First, **Will this congregation continue to engage in God's mission in?** That seems like an obvious no-brainer question but as I travel, I find the answer as lived out in our various congregational contexts is not so obvious. Does your congregation exist to survive or is it actively engaged in God's mission to embody the good news of Jesus Christ in all that we do, say and are? Take time to critically look at your life together both around your kitchen and picnic tables. If your answer is "no" to this question, then hospice chapel status may be a consideration.

Second, **What is the specific/unique mission of this congregation in this community?** What difference does the existence of this congregation make within the life of the parish? If you suddenly no longer existed what would be missing or left undone?

Third, **How will this congregation enact this mission? Please list specific goals.** This is where you look back on your SMART goals. I would suggest choosing between one and three goals for a one-year period. To many goals and you become overwhelmed. Be critical in your choices. Which goals will have the greatest impact in God's mission in your parish?

Fourth, **What resources (financial, pastoral, time) will be needed?** As you look at your SWOT Analysis what are the costs (obvious and hidden) as you look at working on these goals? What resources do you have at your disposal and what partnership will be necessary? As we discussed above, God's mission is bigger than just the work of the congregation.

Final Thoughts

After all of this I find myself back on my Front Porch pondering some tough questions, not the least of which is: Where is the church going? It's not a new question. In fact, much of what follows I wrote 25 years ago.

Where is the church going?

It is a question that I have found on a lot of people's lips recently. It is a question of pastors and congregations alike. I have heard it from thriving as well as struggling congregations. It is the theme of many speculative works of scholarship long on diagnosis but short on prognosis. It is an anxious question that cannot be swept aside. It has been my question this summer as again I prayerfully consider our future together.

It is the consensus of most religious observers worldwide that the age of Christendom, the age of a state-sanctioned and supported church is dead. It is ironic that it is in the country that sought to make no such ties between church and state that its death is last to be noticed. The notion of these United States being a "Christian nation" was alive and well through the last century. As we find ourselves in the 21st Century few evidences of that identity can be readily found in the mainstream of our society. While recent surveys show a majority of people who believe in "god" that god may be Father, Son & Holy Spirit (Trinitarian), Yahweh (Jewish), Allah (Muslim), Buddha (Buddhist) or a plethora of cosmotic gods and personal deities, participation in organized worshipping communities is at a low. We can debate whether the death of Christendom is for the better or worse but that the church as we have known it for the last 1500 years is now in the later stages of *rigor mortis.*

Many churches are busy denying this development by vainly trying to resuscitate a corpse. They have "rediscovered" evangelism, they have produced smorgasbord liturgies, they have pumped money into stewardship and fund raising, they have restructured, and they have designed innovative programs. Yet such CPR is only prolonging and denying the inevitable. We cannot go back nor do I think it would be best for the church to try to go back even if we could.

The acceptance of Christianity by Emperor Constantine gave Christianity legitimacy and an avenue to grow though out the Roman Empire. The cost paid over the centuries was high. Politics and religion have become strange and strained bedfellows. The faith has been compromised, seduced, and aborted more than once for the good of the body politic. In the words of the Civil Rights movement of the 60's, "We are free, we are free at last!"

This freedom is a scary moment in the history of Christianity and the church. Is the church as well as Christendom dead? Hardly! Out of death comes new life. From Good Friday comes Easter morning. This end of Christendom signals a new birth for the church.

Few scholars, however, are willing to speculate on the nature of this resurrected body. What it will look like, how it will act or what its structures will be. Presumptuous as it is of me, I ask for your indulgence as I share with you some of my visions for the future of the church. I hope in the days and years to come this will feed our discussions as we move together into God's future.

The effects of the death of Christendom will not be felt among all churches or structures in the same way. Some will be confronted by its realities quickly; others may stave them off for some time. Some elements of the church may experience the pangs before others. I do believe the whole church will be changed dramatically in the next generation.

The model for this church is not revolutionary but rather grows out of the biblical understanding of God's chosen people. The church is called to be **pilgrim.** A church that is at one and the same a church in transition and a church going somewhere. From the call of Abraham, Isaac and Jacob, through Moses and the prophets, the disciples and apostles God's people were more of a movement (often quite literally) and less of an institution. It is when God's people try to domesticate or institutionalize God that all hell breaks out. The pilgrim church will fight the temptation to give into rigid structures and programs. It will be a church that can respond quickly to the changing times in which we live that will endure. Institutions move like dinosaurs (and often end up like them). The seven last words of the church, "We've never done it like that before!" will be its epitaph. We must believe and trust in the Holy Spirit's guidance. We are after all a people called to walk by faith. As inheritors of grace we are afforded mistakes. We can move boldly! The church that backs into the future will probably get kicked.

This pilgrim church is not only a church on the move, but it is a church going somewhere. God did not leave Moses and the people aimlessly wandering in the desert. He was with them in a pillar of cloud by day and a pillar of fire by night. God will lead us forward as he reconciles us and the world unto himself. It is this reconciliation, begun in Christ that we are called to envision and embody as the church. It is this vision that must always be before us as we make our decisions along the way. The church of tomorrow cannot be everything to everyone- it is called to be the reconciling instrument of Christ in this world. In Hebrew this reconciliation is called, *shalom*. For the Christian it is the inbreaking of the Kingdom of God in Christ.

Inherent in this vision are issues of peace and justice (both political and economic), grace and forgiveness, creator and creature. It impacts the church's life at every turn: preaching, worship, evangelism, stewardship, social ministry and education. Our preaching needs to be that which invites, gathers, educated the world into and about the unfolding age of shalom. It must be biblical and Christ-centered. It cannot succumb to the temptation to avoid the cross in an effort to get to the gospel. Such preaching that advocates a baptism of the cultural values is neither helpful nor faithful. Reconciliation cannot be found without repentance – without turning around to God's activity in our lives and in the world.

Our preaching needs to be that which invites, gathers, and educates the world into and about the unfolding age of *shalom*. It must be biblical and Christ-centered. It cannot succumb to the temptation to avoid the cross in an effort to get to the gospel. Such preaching that advocates a baptism of the cultural values is neither helpful nor faithful. Reconciliation cannot be found without repentance – without turning around to God's activity in our lives and in the world.

The church's worship must maintain its sacramental nature. To speak of reconciliation is to speak of community. The community of the baptized is that body reconciled by God in baptism that struggles daily to live out that reconciliation. It is a community that comes face to face with the Spirit of the risen Christ in the waters of baptism and the flesh and blood reality of the crucified Christ in the Eucharist (Holy Communion). To compromise the integrity of the preached Word and the visible Sacraments is to cheapen the means of grace to that of a vaudeville act. To placate the world's desire to be entertained in worship or for worship to be first and foremost "user-friendly" is nothing short of an abomination! That said we must be ever vigilant in our rites and our worship. Do they speak of reconciliation? Can they speak more proficiently and profoundly? Do they point to God or get stuck in our humanity? As a pilgrim church we must continually look at how we worship that we indeed be faithful bearers of the good news of Jesus Christ.

Evangelism of the church must be beyond the "Field of Dreams Evangelism" of denominationalism. The notions of "Build the right facility...create innovative and alternative worship experiences...have the right programs...offer small groups...show hospitality...put maps up to locate the restrooms... and they will come!" may fill bookshelves in religious book stores and even the pews but it is not the mission of the church. Pilgrim evangelism grows out of worship. As the church is gathered so we are sent. "Come, take and eat...go in peace (*shalom*)." We are thrown back into the world as rudely as Elijah was thrown out of his cozy cave on Mount Horeb. We are called to "serve the Lord" in the task of reconciliation. This kind of evangelism takes place in the trenches of our lives. It is where we live, work and play that we are called to be a reconciling agent for God. It is hard, slow and at times painful work to be a healer. Evangelism should not be a committee but the manifesto of each and every member of the body. It is part and parcel of our baptismal commissioning, "Let you light so shine before others that they may see your good works and glorify the Father." This evangelism is not so much interested in filled pews as it is in new lives.

The task of every Christian in this church, regardless of age, is to wrestle with the question, "What does it mean for me to be a Christian today?" It will be the task of the church's education to provide the arena to assist one another in this struggle. Who we are called to be Christians must be modeled in the liturgy and lived out in the lives of the faithful. To be a pilgrim educator is to acknowledge that we all are in the process of growing in our knowledge of God. As such opportunities for intergenerational learning will be paramount. Education in the church will need the brightest and most creative persons of all ages that the Word may continue to be passed on from generation to generation.

The issues of stewardship and social ministry are intimately tied. Stewardship must get past the idea of supporting the budget to a critical look at how the community of faith uses its resources. It is unconscionable to have over 50% of a church's budget go to staff salaries. The church of the future will have to come to grips with this inequity of stewardship. The focus of the church's financial and human resources will be the care and service of those so easily forgotten. It will be a church called to care for those in need. It will be a church that advocates for justice (reconciliation) in the world as well as the church that staffs the food pantries and soup kitchens. It will be a church found in the volunteer organizations working with the poor, the abused, the handicapped (physically and mentally), the addicted, the homeless and the other faces of Christ in this world.

The church of the kingdom of *shalom* will look differently. It will be a church light on structure and heavy on action. It will need to be a church administered in a way to get things done proficiently. Getting something done will be more important than how it gets done. The church will need to be able to mobilize its resources to meet the growing challenges that face the world. As such, standing committees will give way to task forces and action groups.

The church of the kingdom will be a lay-driven church. It will be a church where all see themselves as members of the body endowed with gifts to offer. The role of the pastor will undergo much evolution (probably kicking and screaming). The office of the ordained minister will no longer be viewed among the many "professionals" of the word but rather a calling out to do a specific ministry – in the Lutheran tradition that will be Word and Sacrament. To preach and preside is to be as Luther called them, the resident bishops- those called to serve and guard the good news. As such theological education will continue to be imperative but it may be more continual than to occur in a four-year stint. The office of pastor will cease to be a full-time paid position. This may not happen in our lifetime, but it will be moving in that direction. A return to the tent-making ministry of Paul will more than likely be the model. The pastor will have another perhaps complementary vocation but will in addition be called to serve the gospel as one set aside for the task of preaching and administering the sacraments.

Some final thoughts on the church catholic. The ghetto mentality of denominationalism will have to give way to a new understanding of the church catholic. The "polite" ecumenism of the last decade will need to be replaced with earnest dialog that neither gets hung up on irreconcilable differences or tries to make a watered-down church where differences are overlooked. This dialog cannot end only in words and agreements but must permeate the life of the congregations. How we act as the church catholic will greatly affect our witness to the world.

The day of the superpower organization of the national and regional church will come to an end soon - quicker where funding streams are more voluntary in nature. The church must flip its flow of ministry from congregation to national church to vice versa. The synodical and churchwide "expressions" must see themselves as servants to the congregation. What can they provide to enable congregations to be faithful in their calling of reconciliation must be the governing question? As such large staffs will not be necessary. The office of the bishop must also be seen as more that of a resident theologian and less that of a fire marshal. (Perhaps a volunteer fire department can be assembled of those equipped for such duty).

Recently, I sat in a darkened and empty church before worship began. A hundred years ago my ancestors brought Lutheranism to this corner of the city. Now the church is being inhabited by another ethnic-specific congregation. Soon they too will vacate this corner. As I sat in that empty church that morning, I was struck by the fact that the Presence Light had burned out. For how long? God only knows! As I reflected on that image I began to wonder, "Has God left the building?" Has God tired of our worn-out liturgies and our tiresome and tedious arguments over the trivial? Is the church of the kingdom of *shalom* a church without walls? As I look around to the world of the streets, I find a hunger for things spiritual that I have ceased to encounter in our religious institutions. Are we being called out of our "God-in-a-box" churches to follow an unleashed God? Is God calling us off Front Porches and our well-set tables to go and be the church – to set the tables in the world that those who have never heard the Word of hope and love and grace may hear and see it in, with and through us?

Several years ago, I received an invitation from Faith Lutheran Church in White Oak, Pennsylvania outside of Pittsburgh. It seems that they had been using my Front Porchin' materials for a couple of years and wanted to have the opportunity to dialog with the author. It turned out to be a ruse. Their intent was to say thank you and to share their story.

It seems that they had been waiting for a new pastor so that they could have a Bible Study. When the new pastor arrived and received the request, he responded much like Jesus did when the disciples wanted him to feed the multitude: You do the Bible Study. The leader panicked at first and then remembered attending one of my Front Porchin' workshops in Pittsburgh. She realized that she had all she needed to do Bible Study in a new way.

A small group began meeting on Tuesday mornings and worked through the list of suggested Bible stories. The group grew and soon people from other congregations were joining them. Soon 20-30 people were gathering every Tuesday to read scripture and to share and deepen their faith. After the first year they developed their own list of material centering around the parables of Jesus.

When I met with them, they spent the morning sharing their personal stories of spiritual transformation and the dramatic change that they had witnessed in the congregation. But most powerful was this story:

It seems that one morning a woman stumbled into the church from off the street. Her life was a train wreck. When she saw cars in the parking lot and decided to reach out to the pastor for help. The pastor was not in. But the Bible Study group was. Since they had spent a year teaching each other how to be present and to share their stories of faith they were ready. Without hesitation, they invited the woman into the group, took care of her immediate needs and surrounded her with God's love and grace. She came back the next week and is now an active worshipper in that congregation.

Thank you for taking the time to sit with me on my Front Porch and wrestle with these difficult issues. Where did we begin? Oh yes, Chris. Thirty years ago, Chris was an exception, today he is the norm. We can remain silent no longer, for the sake of the Chris' of this world and for the world itself. In short, doing evangelism, sharing the good news of Jesus, being missional is not for the sake of the church but for the sake of the world.

We have been given the pearl of great price and we sit on it like an egg. No matter how long we sit on it, no matter how long we talk about, no matter how much we conjecture what we should do with it, it will not hatch. The worth of the experience of Jesus the Christ is revealed only when we share it with others. The question for us today is... What are we waiting for?

APPENDIX A

EXCURSUS ON EXILE

Exile: The New Normal

My ancestors were the first white settlers in the part of Southwestern NY that I called home. Over the course of a few decades they became lumber barons, amassing a fortune in the timber industry. They owned sawmills, a railroad, huge tracts of land as well as a lucrative trade of raw logs which they floated down the Allegheny River to Pittsburgh.

At the turn of the 20th Century the lumber market crashed. While the fortune was lost the memory wasn't. As I look back over the course of the last three generations since then, I realize that my great aunt, Marie (whose life spanned those three generations) took it upon herself in each generation to groom the next Messiah for when "the Lord would restore our family fortunes like the watercourses of the Allegheny."

I was to be my generation's offering. She taught me all the social graces, we dined in fine restaurants, we ate foods that my mother would never have allowed at our table, as she drank her Manhattan she would insist I have a Shirley Temple and taught me how to nurse a drink over the course of a meal. She took me to visit her friends and taught me how to interact with adults (especially those above my station), she introduced me to art, literature and music, but above all she insisted that I could be whatever I wanted to be and that I was destined for greatness.

Throughout my childhood and into young adulthood (she died when I was 27) she continued to coach me. She continually monitored my romantic interests (worried that a girl would come along and take advantage of my gifts and keep me from my destiny). She followed intently my academic endeavors making frequent suggestions about class and career choices. She was excited when I was accepted to an exclusive liberal arts college and as my vocational path turned to the ministry her Roman Catholic heart burst with pride.

It was there at Gettysburg College that all her preparations seemed to pay off. I was now rubbing shoulders with a whole new level of society (one of my fraternity brothers was the son of the CEO of IBM). At every turn those seeds which Marie had planted were being watered by a culture that continually reminded me that I was one of the chosen few.

It was in college that I realized for the first time that I was the last of my Aunt Marie's Messiahs. First her brother, then my uncle and now me. The dark side of Messiahship seemed to be that the previous ones became alcoholics and I was coming to grips with my own drinking habits.

Little did I realize that I was being raised in exile, removed from the land that once was, and living in a foreign land waiting for the return. As I have grown older I realized that the image of the exile is an appropriate descriptor of the spiritual state of much of the region of Northern Appalachia in grew up in and in which I live (perhaps most of the rest of the country as well). What once was is no longer, yet we still remember it and yearn for those days. Days when railroads crisscrossed the territory. Days when heavy industry and manufacturing occupied a place in almost every town. Days when most people enjoyed the same standard of living... not rich but comfortable. A day when kids grew up and took their place next to their parents on the assembly line or in the family business. A day when your neighbors were third and fourth generation residents. A time when we knew each other's stories and we cared for one another in time of crisis. A time when we knew only one or two people that didn't go to church. It was a time when we were **not** concerned about the future. No tinkering! - the present is working good enough. Leave it alone. The only person I ever heard raise a contrary voice was my father. He was a union steward for the railroad and he saw the collapse of the rail industry coming if things did not change. He would return from union meetings enraged that no one else, labor or management, seemed to see or care.

The generation that remembers those days best is fast passing away. My generation, while remembering those days took our parent's advice and fled for greener pastures and promising futures (some of us never made it over the fence). These days we comment on our town and high school Facebook pages with our nostalgic laments.

What causes me despair is not that those days are gone (they were never as good as we think they were) but rather what is left behind. We have become like those by the rivers of Babylon who have forgotten how to sing our songs and tell our stories.

Without them, despair rushes in.

Gone with the railroads, the industry, the educational institutions, the small towns, is the spirit that built and sustained this region. It has been replaced by deep despair and resignation. I refer to it as "systemic stagnation". Attempts to move forward are often met with great resistance. The system that has now taken control is one that benefits most from the status quo (even if it is toxic and sick). In my county, 4 of the top 5 leading employers are mental health companies and facilities.

Our economy is service driven today which benefits from a steady market of sick and needy consumers. This has produced not only despair but also entitlement. When my brother lost his last job, I asked him how his job search was going. He smiled and said he had gotten on with the state of NY. I said, that's great. He laughed and said, "Sure is, they pay me to sit home watch tv and drink beer... life is good." Or the young girl who replied to my wife's encouragement to better her situation by staying in school, "That's not my plan. I'm going to find a guy, get knocked up, have four or five kids, and collect welfare for the rest of my life. It works for mom!"

The pervasiveness of this despair and entitlement and the complicity of the systems leaves me with little hope and trust and a lot of fear for the future of the region. Adding to my despair is the fact that our region's greatest export are our young people. As parents these days we pray that our kids will find good jobs somewhere else (just not too far away). Two of my three children have set down roots in this region which makes me proud and scared to death at the same time.

The drug crisis (which is the new cause *de jour* of all our troubles) is but a symptom of that deep despair. It is not an accident that the most popular drugs in our region are those that either dull pain (opioids) or give one the false sense of self-worth (meth-amphetamine).

Where I do see some hope is in those who are returning from the land beyond. Drawn back by the sacred soil out of which they came they are establishing micro-businesses and cottage industries...creative new ventures. They are infusing new life. New dreams. Perhaps in time, even hope!

There are also the crazy ones like me who love and believe in this place, who came back and refuse to leave. However, I am finding a new wave of burnout among these colleagues. More and more are leaving, tired of watching congregations, businesses and communities disappear before them. (in the last ten years my congregation has lost 55% of its worshipping membership – and they have not all died... they have left). Those of my colleagues that are sticking it out are saying, "I never thought I'd get to this point, but I don't think I can stay here after retirement... it is destroying me."

What keeps me going is that I truly believe that the faith community has a critical role to play in the future if we are willing to endure in hope. By that I do not mean what occurred at our recent ministerium meeting. We brought in the county commissioners and our state representative to talk about how we can form new partnerships to address the issues we are facing in our community and the region. Essentially the message we received from them and the one many of my colleagues were all too eager to receive was, "If we could just get Jesus back to where he belongs, in home, school and church, all our problems would go away." (There were those in the time of the Exile that believed if they could just get back to the Torah/Law, life would be ok for the return trip... then they got home and discovered that home was now a Palestinian Appalachia) and they became distraught and disillusioned.

I believe the image of the exile has much to offer us. I have spent a lot of time recently preaching and teaching on the prophets of the exile. Theirs' is a word of hope to a world of disillusionment, a light in the darkness and life out of death. We have a lot that needs to die if we are going to move forward. We have a lot to leave behind if we are going to make the journey home.

As a Lutheran I bleed grace. I find that a very unpopular word in my world these days which says to me I think there is something there also worth pursuing.

For the past year I have been working with a select group of Dreamers (interestingly enough, we all were raised in Appalachia). The project is looking at Holy Saturday as a model for being church in this place today. Caught between the death of Good Friday and the resurrection of Easter Sunday. A world that once was and a new world yet to be born. What are we to do in the tomb of exile we now find ourselves in? So far, the most powerful revelation that has emerged from the group is the question "How do we sing the doxology in the darkness."

I believe this is not a time to abandon our songs, either our sacred or secular. Our challenge is how do we dare to sing those songs of Zion by the Rivers of Babylon, by the rivers of Appalachia and the many rivers and streams of our land

APPENDIX B

SEASONAL COMMITTEE STRUCTURE

Seasonal Committee Structure

Harold "Jake" Jacobson
Grace Lutheran Church
Clarion, PA

Introduction

The church is today facing a severe resource crisis. It's most valuable and at times most depleted resources are its leaders. Nowhere is this more evident than in the small and mid-sized churches.

I believe that we have compounded our frustrations with this problem because we have turned to business for our models of structure. The corporate model that sets up a board of directors (church council) and committees and sub-committees designed around specific tasks (worship, evangelism, stewardship, social ministry, etc...) may not be our best alternative today. Instead of business models why not look within our own tradition for models. We structure our calendar year around for worship and program around a seasonal calendar which functions very differently than that of the secular world. Why not structure our organizational life around that same calendar.

Much of what follows is the result of an ongoing conversation with the Rev. Dr. John Westerhoff III, former Professor of Religion and Education at Duke University Divinity School, in which he raised the issue and I have tried to provide a working structure to address it.

Rationale

1. How to best utilize the talents and gifts of a limited number of human resources and still provide quality programming and vision.
2. How to creatively live out the story of Christ and the church as we have structured it through the liturgical church year.

Proposal

The proposed structure is designed to be flexible and adaptable to a variety of congregational settings and ways of operating. It takes a little time to feel your way through it in terms of what will work in your setting.

The first step is to determine what committees need to function as standing committees throughout the year.

Next determine how best to group the church calendar year. You may choose to establish a committee for each season. We found that a bit too ambitious as a starting point. We settled on the following:

Advent/Christmas/Ephiphany
Lent/Holy Week/Tridium/Easter
Pentecost/Ordinary Time (we ended up dividing this into a summer and fall component)

We found that the activities and themes of these seasonal groupings flowed nicely one into another.

Committee Agenda

The most important element in this structure is careful homework and planning. I cannot emphasize this enough.

The agenda is developed for two purposes: education and program development

The first item on the agenda is a brief **history of the season and its**

historical themes. Dr. John Westerhoff's book, *A Pilgrim People*, is a valuable resource with this element. The question which needs to grow out of this step and be kept in mind throughout the remainder of the planning is, "What is the church trying to say about God, Christ, and the work of the Holy Spirit through the people of God in this season?"

Reflection on this question should lead to a particular **theme** or direction for your committee at this particular time. The transition is hermeneutical. There needs to be a transition from the historical interpretation of the season to the parish context (What are the needs and concerns that are raised or addressed by this season?). A word of caution needs to be raised in establishing a theme for the season. We have found that some years the theme leaps out at us while at other times we struggle. We have found that if a seasonal theme does not become evident quickly that by proceeding with the planning an appropriate theme often reveals itself.

The most appropriate place to begin the actual planning is with **worship.** This is facilitated by identifying the special worship events which will take place throughout the particular season and also any additional worship events that might be highlighted.

Example: *In the Lenten season one would identify: Ash Wednesday, Passion Sunday, Maundy Thursday, Good Friday as appropriate special celebrations. One might also wish to include special midweek Lenten services to enhance or complement these services.*

This portion of the agenda calls for considerable time. This can be aided by some preplanning on the chairperson's part or by delegating different people to take charge of mini-planning sessions to work out specific details for specific worship events. It has been my experience that it is well worth the time to deal with the final worship portion of the agenda as a group as it allows for a more inclusive expression and flow between worship events.

Included in the worship life of the season might be: hymns, special music, choir, musicians, banners or other art forms, children's sermons, temple talks, bulletin inserts and sermon direction.

You will need to tailor the remainder of your agenda to fit the season, your congregation and the members of your committee.

Learning concerns might include: How can the Sunday School effectively reflect the theme in its lessons? What special educational events (short-term classes or all-day events) might be appropriate? Are there intergenerational or family events that can be reflected in the newsletter, bulletin or internet?

Social Ministry concerns might include: special community projects (health kits, quilting, clothing drive, toy collection, adopt-a-family, adopt-a-grandparent, hat/mitten tree, etc.), special synodical emphasis (advocacy concerns, support of a social ministry agency, etc.).

It is often tempting to treat **Evangelism** within this structure (or any other) very lightly but it has been our experience that when we focused hard on what a particular season had to say to the unchurched of the community we were greatly rewarded. Questions for discussion might include: Are there special areas of evangelical outreach that need to be highlighted during this season? What publicity does there need to be for events and worship?

Stewardship questions could include: What stewardship education needs to be done during this season? What specific gifts are we going to need from the congregation (money for support of specific ministries, talents for specific projects and/or additional time for work in the church, worship or education)?

Community Building concerns need to be shaped around the particular needs of the congregation. In some congregations community building happens best in the context of worship. In others it is in educational events. For still others it is in fellowship and dinner events. Included in the planning should also be a concern for specific groups such as sick, shut-in, inactives and actives. As part of a college community a special concern for community with college students is an important part of our planning.

Youth and other organizations (women's groups, couple's groups, men's groups, etc. can play an important part in implementing projects and facilitate community building. What special projects or events can the groups of the congregation take part in that will reflect the season.

Committee Membership

One of the positive aspects of this structure is that it enables persons with several interests of expertise to fully share these gifts. When you recruit for the committees you need to make sure that you spread these people out over different committees. You will also find that specific people relate more comfortably with one season or another. You will need to have people that can serve as liaisons with musicians, Sunday School teachers and representatives from other organizations within the congregation. It is also helpful if these committees are reflective of the diversity of the congregation.

APPENDIX C

ONE ON ONE
CONVERSATIONS

Domestic Mission
Evangelical Lutheran Church in America

I. PURPOSE - ONE TO ONE VISITS ARE USED TO:

Build Relationships

Relationships cultivate possibilities. It is through relationships that significant things happen. When people are in relationship they can share, plan, dream, create and get things done. Without relationships, people are powerless. People are more likely to respond to an invitation to work together from someone with whom they have a relationship. One to ones build networks of relationships and build community.

Uncover Self Interests

Self interests are those things that a person feels most strongly about. It is the thing that motivates a person. It is their passion or unforgettable fire. People are most likely to get involved in things around their self interests.

<u>Develop Clarity</u>

One to ones allow people to express their feelings about things. When people talk about something, it helps to make that thing clearer to them. People rarely have an opportunity to express themselves to a good listener. A visit provides this opportunity and helps people to gain clarity for themselves. In addition, helping someone develop clarity about what they do strengthens the relationship.

<u>Gather Information</u>

One to ones are an opportunity to gain information about the community, neighborhood, organization, and campaign. You will find out what is going on, where there are overlaps in your lives, and most importantly what people are thinking and feeling.

II. ARRANGING A VISIT AND PREPARATION

The Phone Call

A. A typical visit will be arranged by phone. On the phone you only want to get the appointment. You cannot build a relationship over the phone. To build a relationship you must to sit down and talk with people.

B. Introduce yourself; explain what you are doing and ask if you can have 45 minutes of time to get their point of view.

Example:

"Hi! My name is _____ *and I am on the* _____ *Committee of* _____ *(your organization). As a leader of our campaign to* _____, *I am doing some visits with people to <u>listen</u> to their ideas and learn what is most important to them. Could I arrange to have 45 minutes of your time to <u>listen</u> to your ideas?*

C. Be specific about a day and time, and let them know you only want 45 minutes to an hour of their time. "Can you meet sometime next week? Is it best during the day or in the evening? What works best for you?"

D. Leave it simple and general, and make it clear that you are coming to hear their ideas, and not to <u>sell</u> them on anything.

Before the visit, take time to prepare. Think about what you may know about the person or what they are involved in. Review what you think may be their self interest. Think through what questions you want to be sure to ask, and what you say about what you are doing.

III. THE VISIT

There is no formula for having a good visit. Enjoy yourself and try to establish some rapport. Here are some general points that may help you do this:

<u>Introduce Yourself And Explain Why You Are There</u>

(Same as telephone explanation)

<u>Warm Up</u>

Have a few simple questions or comments ready to develop a little relaxed conversation at the beginning. This will get them talking and help you get a feel for them. Ask questions, listen closely, keep it relaxed. Talk about things the person seems interested in.

<u>Listen Intently, Especially for "Lead-Ins" To Stories</u>

Getting them talking is important. Speak in order to draw them out. A successful visit means the person visited is speaking <u>70%</u> of the time, and most people are flattered when you show an interest in them and their opinions.

Stories tell the most and are usually more enjoyable than abstractions. Probe for specifics about their experiences and their true feelings about things.

Some areas that can be explored are:

anger	ambitions/dreams	reading
history	organizations	politics
religion	job	hobbies
education	values	
community	family	

Seek To Identify Self-Interests - Be Courageous

Listen to hear what seems to excite and/or motivate them. Gather enough specifics about their actual behavior to see if your hunches about their self interest are born out. Use follow-up questions for more detail, to stimulate the conversation. Follow your own curiosity. Be courageous. Probe by asking "WHY?".

Establish Some Common Ground

Share some things about yourself and your experiences. Especially seek to find some common ground, if it is there. We are promising people that we just want to listen to their point of view.

We are not selling anything.
We are not recruiting anyone for a project.
We are not preaching to them.
We are not judging or psychoanalyzing them.

If you find yourself doing these things – stop!

Ask Who Else You Should Visit

Ask who else you should talk to. Who might have similar perceptions? Different ones? Can you use their name when contacting them? If someone asks what you want to talk to others about, the answer is, "The same things you and I talked about."

Establish A Follow-up, If Appropriate

If the person interested you and you see some opportunity for a next step, set up that expectation before you leave. "This was very interesting. I would like to call you in a couple of weeks and schedule some time to talk more about our campaign." If you did not find overlapping self-interests, do not set up expectations.

Close the Visit

Watch the time so that you do not spend too long – 45-60 minutes is enough. End the visit by thanking the person for their time.

V. REFLECTION AND EVALUATION

After a visit fill out the reflection form. (Do not fill out the form during a visit.) It is important for you to reflect on the visit, think about what they said and what it really meant, and what you did and why. You cannot keep all this in your head, and the next time you visit or talk to them, you will have these notes to refresh your memory.

Some questions that will help you reflect on a person's self interest:

- What does this person care most about? Why?
- What motivates them?
- What do they get excited talking about?
- How do they spend their time?
- What talents and abilities does this person have?
- How and where are they using them?
- What relationships does this person have and value? Why?
- What specific concerns or ideas does this person have?
- What is this person's story?
- Why is this person involved in the things they're involved in?

Evaluate yourself. Ask:

- Did I establish a relationship?
- How well did I uncover self interest?

- How courageous was I? What was the riskiest question I asked?
- What did I do well?
- What could I have done differently?

ONE-ON-ONE REFLECTION

Person Visited:_____Phone_____

E-mail Address:_____

A. **Important things I learned about this person:**

_____

_____

_____

_____

_____

_____

B. **Talents, background, and/or gifts this person has to offer:**

_____

_____

_____

_____

_____

C. **What are this person's areas of "<u>self interest</u>"?**

_____

_____

_____

_____

_____

_____

Questions For Reflection While Considering the questions on the other side:

<u>Relationship</u>:
What do we have in common? What might be the basis of a relationship?

<u>Self Interest</u>:
What does this person care most about? Why?
What do they get excited talking about?
How do they spend their time?
What talents and abilities does this person have?
How and where are they using them?
What relationships does this person have?
What specific concerns or ideas does this person have? Why?
What is this person's story?
Why is this person involved in the things they're involved in?
Is there a potential role in the campaign that would really get them excited?

Self Evaluation:

_____

_____

_____

_____

_____

Questions to reflect on:

What did I do well?

What can I do differently next time?

Did I establish a relationship?

Did I listen for the stories behind people's facts and opinions?

How courageous was I? Did I probe?

What was the riskiest question I asked?

Were there "leads" that they gave me that I didn't follow up? Why?

APPENDIX D

SWOT ANALYSIS

Internal	
Strengths	Weaknesses
1.	

External	
Opportunities	Threats
1.	

SWOT Analysis Summary

APPENDIX E

THEOLOGY OF EVANGELISM

Quest for a Theology of Evangelism in the New Normal

Harold "Jake" Jacobson
COVID -19, 2020

For the first 25 years of my ministry I was challenged by parishioners, colleagues, synod and churchwide staff to do the work of an evangelist. For the last 12 years I have been appointed the resident expert on our synod territory for all things pertaining to evangelism. All of this has carried with it the subtle (okay, not so subtle) message that I needed to be about evangelism if the church was going to survive. As, then Presiding Bishop Mark Hanson informed us when he appointed us as Directors for Evangelical Mission, "We are betting the farm on you!" It doesn't get much more blatant than that.

Through it all no one had adequately offered up a theological reason for doing evangelism that did not sound, in my most gracious moments, "self-serving" and on my bad days, "prostituting the gospel for the sake of the institution." If our aim for evangelizing is not (as our "evangelical" brothers and sisters insist) to save souls for Jesus, then what is it?

I met Chris his first year at Clarion University of PA at a midsemester cookie break sponsored by campus ministry. He was there with his roommate who had become a regular at Grace's worship. Chris and I hit it off from the moment we met. We found connections and mutual interests galore. We sat and talked for several hours. On my way back home, I remarked to myself that

I would probably see Chris in church on Sunday. (I was still young and naïve enough to believe that people came to church because of the pastor – age and experience has changed that thinking).

That Sunday there was no Chris. Weeks went by, months went by, semesters went by, years went by and still no Chris. We met regularly on campus and we saw each other in town but never in church. Then on the last Sunday of his senior year I looked up and saw Chris and his roommate sitting in the back pew. I figured he came just to say goodbye.

You can imagine my surprise when the following Sunday he was there without his roommate. He had also hung behind after service to talk with me. "Pastor, I want to join the church." Somewhat shocked, I replied, "Give me a call this week and we can set up a time to get started on the process." He didn't call.

The next week he was waiting for me after church once again. "Pastor Jake, I needed to tell you something, but I couldn't do it over the phone. I'm kind of embarrassed … I've never been baptized." "That's ok, baptism will be the way we welcome you into the church. Give me a call this week and we can set up a time to get started on the process." He didn't call.

Chris was not there the next Sunday, or the Sunday after that, or the Sunday after that. In fact, Chris seemed to be MIA. I figured I must have said something to scare him off or upset him. About the time I had given myself a good beating up there he was waiting for me after church. "I bet you wondered what happened to me?"

"I decided that if I wanted to become a Christian, I should make sure what kind of Christian I wanted to be. So, I visited all the churches in town. I want to be a Lutheran Christian."

"Fine, be in my office tomorrow morning at 9:00." He was.

We began to talk about his story and how he had gotten to Clarion and how he had come to his decision to join the church. I began to talk about the Bible, sharing some of the important stories. He hung with me through the Old Testament but as we reached the New Testament, he became more agitated. I noticed it, but since he was my first adult baptism and I had so much good stuff I wanted to share, I kept plowing on until he had had enough. "Pastor Jake, shut up, I have a question. You keep talking about this Jesus guy. Who is Jesus?"

The interesting piece about Chris's question was that he was not interested in learning about who Jesus was. He wasn't looking for information about Jesus, a kind of Jesus 101. He had not been impressed by our music ministry, our warm and friendly community, or my sermons. He wanted to encounter the Divine One that he saw in his roommate and others. He now could put a name to it… "Introduce me to this Jesus".

The backstory to Chris' showing up at church that first Sunday hits at our quest.

It was the week between finals and college graduation. He and his roommate were sharing an adult beverage and discussing the next chapter in their respective lives. Chris said that he had achieved all of the goals he had set for himself and the next chapter was already set in motion (Graduate School). However, he found a great hole in his life, an emptiness that he could not fill, a yearning that would not be satisfied. He turned to his roommate and asked him if he could help him get rid of the hole. His roommate simply said, "No." "What I can tell you is that when I start feeling that emptiness and yearning, I go to church. I do not know what happens to me there, but I do know that when I leave the hole is smaller, the emptiness bearable and the yearning actually comforting. Do you want to go to church with me tomorrow?"

… and you know the rest of the story.

What Chris encountered at Grace was the presence of the God we have come to call, Father, Son and Holy Spirit, AND he wanted more! Is not this why we do evangelism? Is it not the sharing of the story of Jesus in such a way that it invites the hearer into a deeper relationship with God? Is it not that they may find grace upon grace and life abundant? As such evangelism *is* our ministry both to those who know the story well as well as to those who have never heard.

If we are not inviting people into a deeper relationship with the living God (and deepening that relationship among those already in the gathered body) then what do we have to offer those we seek to "evangelize"? Is it a community? Is it an entertaining event? Is it a charismatic pastor? Is it uplifting and inspiring music? Is it programming for their children and youth? Is it service to the community?

Even our best evangelism language falls short. "We seek to evangelize others so that they may become part of the body of Christ". Can we incorporate people into the body of Christ without introducing them to the crucified and risen God? Can we expect them to remain if we do not help them deepen that relationship?

I believe the problem is in part our starting point. We begin with the Great Commission and not the Great Commandment. When we begin our evangelism efforts with the Great Commission we begin with *our* call/work. As such we do something to others: baptize, make disciples and teach. If we begin with the Great Commandment, we are inviting others into a relationship with God first, and then the community of faith (neighbor). It's like fishing without an understanding of what to do with the fish once you catch them. Too many of our evangelism efforts end with the great catch of fish on Easter Monday but fail to engage people in Peter's difficult conversation with Jesus over breakfast.

In my reading on church renewal and evangelism I often am told that the congregation must choose what kind of church they want to be. Typically, they site the two main types of church as being those motivated by the Great Commandment churches or the Great Commission churches.

Frankly, I do not think we can pull them apart. But it is important to get the relationship right.

My theological ground zero is the Great Commandment: You shall love the Lord, your God and your neighbor. When I teach or preach this, I use the image of a cross. The vertical is our love of God and our horizontal is our love of neighbor. Where they meet is where I find Jesus. For me, Jesus is first and foremost, the crucified one. As such, Jesus is the one who restores my relationship to God (again and again) and accompanies me (as the Holy Spirit) to love and serve my brothers and sisters. Jesus is not the end of our journey but the beginning, the entry point, of a deeper relationship with God and neighbor.

If we stop with Jesus as friend, then we often make God into a Big Warm Fuzzy. If Jesus is our personal Lord and Savior, then Jesus becomes the carrot to live a virtuous life. Neither of these is satisfactory motivation for evangelism within the Lutheran tradition (not to say that they both are not in existence in our churches).

So, where does that leave us?

Where all good Lutheran theology begins and ends, the cross.

As I am writing this, we are in week six of stay at home orders in the midst of the COVID-19 virus. Systematically, every single one of my props and coping devises has been pulled out from underneath me. I have been left with a hole bigger than Chris', an unbearable emptiness and a relentless yearning. I have found myself driven to the cross again and again.

It is here all of my best (and worst) efforts are exposed as mere folly. All of the pastoral props of ministry that let me dare to believe, "My, you are a righteous and sacrificial pastor" are stripped away and I am left standing naked before that cross. For the first time I am confronted with the vision in the mirror that allows those words of Ash Wednesday to strike deep within me, "You are but dust and to dust you shall return." Luther was right, I am nothing more than fodder for the worms.

The surprise to me has been that this news has not devastated me but opened my eyes to the grace revealed in the death and resurrection of Christ. I have been renewed in my baptismal covenant. Perhaps most shockingly, I have a deep desire to tell others what I have seen and heard in the midst of this empty tomb.

"Go, let your light so shine before others that they may see in you the glory of your Father in heaven." As I read the gospels and as I reflect on our baptismal call, this is our only call, to enable others to know Jesus.

Perhaps this is what drove the likes of Paul and the early evangelists to go into the world making disciples of all peoples, baptizing them in the name of the Father, and of the Son and of the Holy Spirit. Christianity was the only religion in its day that actually went and shared the tenants of its faith with others outside their normal spheres of influence. Which is what got them in trouble with those in authority, both Jews and Romans.

Short of a pandemic, how do we nurture such faith?

One of the things that this pandemic has given us is time and space. Unfortunately, many are doing their best to fill it up and develop the church for the new normal which looks much like a high-tech version of the old normal. The movement to on-line worship has simply made obvious what has been happening for decades. Our worship has become an event. In the struggles of a colleague, "I am having a hard time trying to create a meaningful Easter experience for my people."

Our congregations have a unique opportunity to decide what kind of a church we want to be as we move out of this time of isolation. If we don't take this time to reshape our ministry around the story of Christ crucified and how that has impacted our lives (particularly in the midst of what we are going through) then we will have missed a gift from God. We have seen the impact of our efforts to reach out on-line. Still, if we think that live streaming our worship will fix the church, we will be sorely disappointed. It is time to retool do be the evangelism/missional/vital church we keep claiming that we want to be.

To that end I propose the following questions for us to begin to wrestle with as we move forward:

1. How do we more effectively communicate the gospel of Jesus Christ to the world? (this is where I believe our technology opens endless possibilities for the creative and innovative among us).
2. How do we help people enter into a deeper relationship with the God we know as Father, Son and Holy Spirit?
3. How do we preach, teach, confess and **live** out our theology of the cross and of grace?
4. How do we as rostered leaders in this church begin to understand to role of the Holy Spirit in all of this vis-à-vis our perceived responsibility? (I have realized that this has always been a weakness in Lutheran theology but if we don't get past the notion that this is all up to us – there will be none of us left).
5. How do we listen better to the world around us so that we begin to "hear" the cries of their hearts and lives and not just the superficial whining about needs and wants?
6. How do we become instruments of God's healing after this crisis period is over?
7. How do we move beyond the question, "How do we save this church?" and into "How are we called to be agents of grace and healing to the world?"

Jesus says and demonstrates a great deal about loving God and neighbor but not a whole lot about keeping the institution afloat. Something to ponder.